WHY BOTHER WITH
MISSION?

WHY BOTHER WITH
MISSION?

STEPHEN GAUKROGER

Inter-Varsity Press

INTER-VARSITY PRESS
38 De Montfort Street, Leicester LE1 7GP

© Stephen Gaukroger, 1996

Study questions prepared by Phil Cuthbert, © IVP, 1996

First published 1996

British Library Cataloguing in Publication Data
A catalogue record for this book is available from the British Library.

ISBN 0–85111–169–6

Photoset by Parker Typesetting Service, Leicester.

Printed in Great Britain by Cox & Wyman Ltd, Reading.

Inter-Varsity Press is the book-publishing division of the Universities and Colleges Christian Fellowship (formerly the Inter-Varsity Fellowship), a student movement linking Christian Unions in universities and colleges throughout the United Kingdom and the Republic of Ireland, and a member movement of the International Fellowship of Evangelical Students. For information about local and national activities write to UCCF, 38 De Montfort Street, Leicester LE1 7GP.

CONTENTS

FOREWORD

Don't read this book! Stop! Right now, not another word! Well, if you must continue to read on, just read the foreword . . . but nothing else. Okay. Good.

For a start, this book is about spreading the 'good news' all over the world so everyone on the planet has a chance to know God. That is unrealistic, arrogant and unnecessary. Unrealistic: because the church can't even affect the houses around it, so what hope does it have of affecting anywhere else? Arrogant: because we have come to recognize, in the late twentieth century, the need to treat all religions equally and to respect the right of everyone, everywhere, to make their own minds up about everything, without our old-fashioned assumption that we are right! Unnecessary: because through mass communication, Bible translations and the missionaries of past generations, all those who want to know about Christianity can find out without us doing anything else.

And, of course, the subject of mission is

boring! Even if you do begin this book, you'll probably be asleep before you are half-way through chapter two! We have all sat through tedious presentations about God's work among the 'Batutsi' people on the southern rim of an unpronounceable mountain range in an insignificant country with a smaller population than the Orkneys. There are far more exciting things to get involved in.

People in other countries, and the unchurched in this, don't need or want our interference in their lives. God is perfectly capable of getting their attention if he wants to. Remember this wise piece of advice:

Sit down O men of God,
His kingdom He will bring,
Whenever it may please His will;
You cannot do a thing!

The Bible itself says, 'charity begins at home', so let's attend to our own concerns in the church fellowship. We have plenty of problems of our own to keep us occupied. Is everything perfect in your local church? Of course not. Shouldn't we make sure that everyone is mature spiritually, happy emotionally, healthy physically, released 'giftedly' and financially non-challenged, before we even think about mission? Of course we should!

And in all this, remember why I was asked to write this foreword. I know more about mission than almost anyone else. You'd be amazed at the number of countries I've visited and the churches I've influenced over the years. I told Jesus to concentrate on his own needs, not to worry about the whole world. He didn't listen, and everyone knows about the sad consequences of his ignoring me – a cruel early death. I gave Paul a thorny problem to dissuade him from mission – but he went right on planting churches and evangelizing. I warned William Carey about the problems in India and Gladys Aylward about the dangers in China. I told Charles Spurgeon that there were too many orphans for his little orphanage to make any difference. I've lost count of the number of conversations I've had with Billy Graham – is anyone really listening to all those sermons? Not to mention the thousands of unknown evangelists, doctors, agriculturalists, church planters, teachers, pastors, engineers and accountants – every one a missionary – who I've tried to persuade to leave their 'ministry' and get a proper job, in more comfortable surroundings! Even though I've made it clear that their churches have forgotten them and that nobody remembers to pray for them; that they will probably get sick, stay poor, remain unappreciated and die misunderstood, they have refused to give up! I'm not sure what else I can do. Some people just won't take the sensible and safe option.

I have higher hopes for the readers of this book. As we approach the twenty-first century we are becoming much more sophisticated and street-wise. We know better than our predecessors and will not be fooled by a simplistic understanding of the Great Commission. When Jesus said to go into all the world and preach the good news to all creation, he obviously didn't mean what he appears to say. Let's leave the task of world mission to the misguided, the misled and the fanatical. At last in our generation we will get this whole thing under control. You need read no further!

Lucy Fer

Lucy Fer

cha*chapter one*

BECOMING A
WORLD CHRISTIAN

. . . .

'A World Christian isn't better than other Christians. But by God's grace, they have made a discovery so important that life can never be the same again. World Christians are day-to-day disciples for whom Christ's global cause has become the integrating, overriding priority for all that He has for them. Like disciples should, they actively investigate all that their Master's great commission means. Then they act on what they learn.'

David Bryant

. . . .

Every believer in Jesus has the incredible privilege of sharing in his world-plan. This plan excludes no-one; all, without regard to nationality, race, colour or gender, are loved by him. He longs for young and old, rich and poor, from the North Pole to the South Pole, to discover this love. We are called to be co-workers (2 Corinthians 6:1) with God in putting the plan into practice. But how? As we shall see later, although we are called to mission, we are not necessarily being called to another country, or even to 'full-time Christian service' in our own. Yet we are all called to be world Christians. Let's explore what this means, and how we can take practical steps to become one.

For many of us, becoming a world Christian may involve a change in our *attitudes.* Sometimes we live our lives in boxes or compartments. One has the label 'church' and one has the label 'world'. These two boxes are quite separate and distinct. The 'world' is bad and we should avoid contact with it as much as possible. The 'church' is good and we should give time and money to it, while keeping it away from the 'world' so it doesn't become 'worldly'. Of course there is some truth in this – the world can be a very bad place indeed. But this can be a very dangerous view, damaging our missionary impact in the world. It has led some Christians to view their lives from Monday to Saturday in a completely different way to their lives on Sunday. They see God as interested only in the *religious* bits of their lives, not in the *secular* bits, such as work, home and leisure. This has had the tragic effect of producing Christians with a faith which has almost no impact on their everyday lives – a faith which does not affect the way they treat their marriage partner, their colleagues at work, or their relatives. The result of trying to keep these two boxes separate ('church' and 'world') is often to produce worldly Christians, whose behaviour is almost identical to all the non-Christians around them. This has the effect of neutralizing our witness in the very place it is meant to be most potent.

In addition, it has meant an abdication of responsibility in huge sections of modern life. A Christian ghetto claims our presence and our commitment, to the exclusion of the 'bad' world which we want to avoid. Many Christians spend all their time in church activity and meetings. They read Christian books and magazines, go on holiday with other Christians to Christian conferences, while listening to Christian music in the car on the journey there. All their friends are Christians, and, if they could, they would work for a Christian company and send their children to Christian schools. It doesn't take a genius to figure out that this kind of lifestyle is going to make it a little tricky to have a significant Christian impact on our friends and neighbours. Not that any of these things are wrong in themselves – we obviously have our own needs for fellowship and teaching – but we are called to be 'salty' in a bland, tasteless world and 'light' in dark places (Matthew 5:13–16). We can't be these things unless we engage the non-Christian world clearly and consistently. To be a world

Christian means that we do not have the luxury of opting out of contact with those who don't know Jesus.

. . . .

'Every Christian should be a World Christian,
a global disciple, a Great Commission Christian,
a servant of God. But what does this mean?
Three commitments . . . characterise the World Christian
(and should be the characteristic of every Christian).
'World Christians are:

* *Committed to God's purpose for his world.*

* *Committed to God's people who are to carry out his purpose.*

* *Committed to working out God's purpose in daily life.'*

Robin Thomson, *World Christian*
(Lynx/St John's Extension Studies, 1992).

. . . .

This opting out has not just affected our presence but also our influence in the world. Whole areas of modern life have been abandoned in favour of religious activity. Politics, economics, social action, the media, business, education, science, philosophy, the arts – all need 'salty' Christians at the very highest levels.

The fruit of this absence is everywhere. In the issue of the environment, for example, we complain at the influence of New Age thinking, when we should be asking why Christians have been so slow to communicate the biblical position. Concern for creation did not begin with the Green movement (Genesis 2:15; Psalm 8; Matthew 10:29)!

. . . .

'A world-class Christian is one whose lifestyle and obedience are compatible, in cooperation, and in accord with what God is doing and wants to do in our world.'

Paul Borthwick, *How to be a world-class Christian* (Victor Books, 1993), p. 91.

. . . .

World Christians have discovered that holy living is a biblical lifestyle empowered by the Spirit of their living Lord. They are not *of* this world (John 17:15–16) but are definitely *in* it. Up to their necks in it! Shining bright and being salty for Jesus.

How, in practice, can we avoid a 'Christian ghetto' mindset? We can become more aware of the world and its needs by, for example:

* Watching the news or buying a newspaper.

* Occasionally picking up a magazine which looks at the news in a more 'in depth' way.

* Spending time tuning in to a panel discussion on radio or TV rather than watching *Neighbours*.

* Joining a local sports team, night-school class or supper club.

* Participating in a local Neighbourhood Watch scheme or Residents' Association.

* Subscribing to a mission magazine, dealing with work on another continent.

* Becoming a school governor or member of the Parent-Teacher Association at the local school.

* Befriending an international student.

* Learning a foreign language!

* Visiting another country, preferably not a usual holiday destination. Try to stay with local people.

All these things will broaden our horizons and give us insights into the 'world' of people not yet Christian – wherever in the world they may be.

But of course, world Christians want to do more than understand the world; they also want to change it and support others who are trying to change it. Our support can take a number of forms.

PRACTICAL

World Christians are not content to talk about supporting others involved in mission – they do it! We could use a summer vacation to visit a Christian worker in another country. This can be wonderfully encouraging. Many foreign mission personnel have never had someone from their home church visit them. A trip like this supports them and gives us insights we could never get if we stayed at home. We could send small gifts abroad and ask to be sent their prayer/news-letter – even read it! Perhaps we could volunteer to copy and distribute their letters to the rest of the church.

Writing letters to mission workers is a great idea. Correspondence is received with an enthusiasm far in excess of the energy it takes to write it. You may even be able to fax or E-mail it, depending on the resources available to the mission personnel.

How to write a good letter to a Christian worker abroad

* Do not be over spiritual. Write about local news items, sporting highlights or an occasional television programme. Give up-to-date information on 'births, deaths and marriages' in your church, if they are familiar with the church family. Let them know about the humorous incidents too.

* Write on special occasions. Remember to post in good time for anniversaries, birthdays and Christmas. Major occasions can highlight the loneliness when you are away from home.

* Include interesting newspaper or magazine cuttings, a photo of the kids and the church magazine.

* Occasionally send a postcard, perhaps when you are on holiday. It will be encouraging for your missionary friends to be sent invitations to weddings, too, even if you know they will not be able to come. At least they will feel less left out.

* Say you are praying for them (and do it!) and offer a verse from the Bible to encourage them.

* Do not expect a reply to every letter.

* You could experiment with putting a message on cassette or making an annual phone call.

* Be creative! Try to put yourself in their position and respond accordingly.

When we see our workers return we can take them out for a meal or to see a play. We certainly ought to plan to be at least as supportive when they come home as we are when they are away.

PRAYING

What we pray about reveals our priorities (such as health, money, family, good weather). We should pray about mission until it becomes a priority! We may not personally be able to take the good news abroad, but we can all pray in such a way that regions abroad are affected. I believe that individuals, and whole churches, need to rediscover the power of prayer and the sheer thrill of sharing in God's purposes, by praying. Prayer needs no passport, visa or work permit. There is no such thing as a 'closed country' as far as prayer is concerned. It doesn't suffer from jet-lag, language problems or cultural adjustment. It can cross thousands of miles and any number of time zones, penetrate any building, in any weather . . . and all in less than a split second! Prayer is God's strategy for making plain the defeat of his enemies. Much of the history of mission could be written in terms of God moving in response to persistent prayer.

Mission history is filled with stories of Christians feeling compelled to pray at precisely the time when a specific missionary was facing a crisis – completely unknown to the person who felt driven to prayer. Disaster has been averted, death prevented, break-throughs in evangelism seen . . . all in response to prayer. And, no less important, the routine, day-to-day work of mission is sustained through regular, faithful praying. Despite overwhelming opposition, prayer sees God's work continue undefeated. In some parts of the world it is almost impossible to explain the continued presence of Christian missionaries, without acknowledging the role of prayer.

Leaders in mission are often the quickest to admit their need of prayer; and are the greatest believers in its power. Hudson Taylor, for example, was instrumental in seeing God's love released in China. First he prayed for seventy men workers in a year, then a hundred the next, and then a thousand new workers over five years. God answered all these requests; the China Inland Mission was born and this huge nation was exposed to the gospel.

The need for praying people

'I am persuaded that England is rich in godly, quiet, praying people, in every denomination. They may not be a great multitude as far as numbers are concerned, but they are "rich in faith", even if many of them be poor and of humble station. It is the prayers of such that I covet more than the gold of Ophir – those good old men and good old women (yes, and not necessarily old either) who know what it is to have power with God and prevail . . . Will you help me, prayerfully and judiciously, to get some of these to join the circle? . . . The work for which I am asking prayer is the preaching and teaching the Word of God, pure and simple . . . I have no confidence in anything but the Gospel of Calvary to uplift these needy people.'

Letter of James Frazer, missionary to the Lisu people, China. Quoted in *Mountain Rain*, by Eileen Crossman (OMF, 1988).

We can all pray privately for some aspect of mission. This praying should be informed, persistent and expectant. We could join a missionary prayer group, or form a prayer triplet with a world mission as a focus. We could set aside an hour a week to pray specifically for mission.

M I S S I O N ?

. . . .

'The church has many organisers, but few agonisers; many who pay, but few who pray; many resters, but few wrestlers; many who are enterprising, but few who are interceding. The secret of praying is praying in secret. That is the difference between the modern church and the early church. In the matter of effective praying, never have so many left so much to so few. Let us pray!'

Leonard Ravenhill

. . . .

Some Christians plan to fast on one day each month and use the time they would spend on eating by praying for world concerns. Whatever we do we must pray.

Being a world Christian

'It's all right for you to advocate all Christians should be global Christians. You've travelled constantly and from what you've said, you certainly adapt extremely well to new friends and cultures. My world is rather different. I spend more time with animals than with human beings. My wife and I had to summon up extra reserves of courage just to cross the channel for a day trip to France.' Mr Lester was a dairy farmer from Yorkshire and he rarely minced his words. He was visiting his daughter in Southampton and heard me

22

speaking at a missionary weekend. Before I could comment he went on, 'Moreover, your job and your organization force you to be a world Christian. What about ordinary believers like myself?'

I asked him whether he watched the news on TV. 'Of course I do – every day. I carry a small transistor radio with me and I tune to the BBC World Service.' 'That's excellent,' I retorted. 'That's where I get most of my material for global praying.' He looked rather surprised. I explained that national and world news always provided me with splendid opportunities for intercession. At that time the famine in Ethiopia and Sudan was grabbing the headlines. The tragic scenes of poverty, death and misery triggered me to pray for the leaders of both nations, as well as the victims of malnutrition and famine. I showed Mr Lester *Operation World* by Patrick Johnstone. I explained, 'This is an excellent resource book for global Christians. It's packed with concise information on every nation. When a news item strikes me, I consult this book to find out more about the country that's making the news.'

We decided to check out Ethiopia and Sudan. Within minutes we gleaned vital information on both countries. We studied the population figures and compared the relative strength of the church in both countries. We immediately discerned that the Christians in southern Sudan were in the majority, but in the north they were in a minority under the Arabs.

We read useful statistics about the size and influence of the Ethiopian Orthodox Church and its hostility towards Protestants. The prayer requests enabled us to target specific prayers for both nations.
By then Mr Lester was getting rather excited. 'Hey, this is thrilling! I can be a world Christian where I am; my papers and TV news broadcasts can serve as prompts for prayer. Thank you for introducing me to *Operation World* – where can I buy a copy?' Thankfully, he was able to purchase a copy from the church booktable.

Chua Wee Hian, *Getting through customs*
(IVP, 1992), pp. 180–181.

GIVING

God's work needs God's money to be released through God's people. Not all the churches in the New Testament times had grasped this, and Paul himself only seems to have been adequately supported by the Christians in Philippi (Philippians 4:14–18). The church at Corinth needed a reminder to be generous (2 Corinthians 9:5) and Timothy is challenged about the dangers of materialism (1 Timothy 6:6–10). How we need to hear this again today.

As we approach the year 2000 much mission work is in financial crisis. Mission agencies have found themselves making staff redundant, freezing salaries and restricting the development of new projects. Literature remains unprinted; or, if printed, undistributed. Finance for capital expenditure isn't available, so organizations struggle with inadequate premises, out-dated computers and photocopiers, and unreliable vehicles. This makes the organization expensive to run and relatively inefficient. Yet the resources are available if only God's people would release them.

A biblical lifestyle demands generous giving. Perhaps every Christian should have a 'giving goal' toward which they aim. This goal could be something like: 'To give 10% of my income to the local church and 5% of my income to world mission, by five years from now.' No Christian can tell another how much to give, so we must never feel bullied or pressurized. Personal circumstances vary enormously (such as debt, children, employment, savings) but every believer has a responsibility before God to give sacrificially.

It is important to allocate your money as soon as you receive it – weekly or monthly – rather than waiting to see what is left. Some people find it helpful to put it into a simple collecting box on the same day each week or month.

Others give by cheque or standing order at the bank. Don't forget that your church or mission agency can claim your tax back if you sign a Deed of Covenant or Gift Aid form. Some countries have schemes to facilitate giving to charity, such as the Charities Aid Foundation and UKET in the UK. Such excellent ideas will increase the size of your gift significantly. Why not have a chat to your church treasurer, if you need help with this?

THINKING

World Christians will want to engage their brains in trying to understand the complexities of the late twentieth-century international community. (This will be more appealing to some of us than others!) World mission is being faced with some difficult questions: What right do we have to interfere with another country's culture, religion and heritage? Don't missionaries create more problems than they solve (adding to political instability; creating unmet wants and unnecessary dissatisfaction with the status quo)? Why do we need to send missionaries to parts of the world where the church is growing faster than it is in Britain? Some Christians have been so embarrassed by these questions that they have let mission slip off the agenda.

'Anthropologists identify the earliest stages of societies as "hunters and gatherers", those people who have foraged through the fields and forests gathering berries and roots and other edibles for their sustenance. I like to think of world-class Christians as "hunters and gatherers" in a different way. To further our growth, we are always hunting for information and gathering data about issues in the world into which God calls us. We continue to grow by foraging through books, newspapers, and a host of other sources to expand our minds concerning God's great world.'

Paul Borthwick, *How to be a world-class Christian*
(Victor Books, 1993), p. 24.

But if we want our Christian faith to be thoughtful and consistent, we will meet these questions head-on. The good news is that while these may be new questions to us, most of the best mission agencies have been grappling with them for a long time. In fact, criticism of foreign missionaries goes back a long way. Almost two hundred years ago, at the start of the nineteenth century, the British East India Company said, 'The sending of Christian Missionaries into our eastern possessions is the maddest, most expensive, most unwarranted project that was ever proposed by a lunatic enthusiast!' However, by the close of the nineteenth century, a hundred years later, the Governor of Bengal was saying, 'In my judgment, Christian missionaries have done more lasting good to the people of India than all the other agencies combined.'

It is worth asking these same 'difficult' questions about Islamic or Hindu mission and missionaries. Do you think asking these questions will slow down the building of mosques in non-Islamic countries? (All those who answer Yes to this question – I have some land on Jupiter to sell you!) Why don't other countries give the same freedom to Christianity which we give to their predominant religion? And perhaps we send missionaries to Brazil and Korea (where church growth is rapid) because they still ask us to! Often where there are thousands of new converts there is a huge need for leadership training, advice on pastoral care and teaching on discipleship. What we learn in these situations we can bring back home to reinvigorate the western church. And we do have a great deal to learn from the rest of the world. Almost three quarters of all evangelical Christians now live in the 'two-thirds' world. Britain, for instance, could soon be receiving more missionaries than it sends abroad. World mission gives us a great opportunity to get involved in what God is doing on every continent – receiving just as much as we contribute to others.

So the next time there is a rather cynical documentary about missionaries on the television or an article in the newspaper – don't worry! Perhaps you could write down the questions which trouble you and send them to a mission agency, asking for their response. Alternatively, ask your local Christian bookshop for some material, or talk to your minister, or to a missionary on home assignment. There are good, satisfying answers to these questions!

CHAPTER ONE

BECOMING A WORLD CHRISTIAN

KEY PASSAGE

John 4:27–38

QUESTIONS FOR DISCUSSION

1 'A world Christian is someone who . . .'. Using this chapter, draw up a definition of a world Christian. Do this as a group, or in threes, feeding back your definitions to come up with a composite.

2 On pages 19–20 we read of praying, giving and thinking as a world Christian. Which of these is your strongest, and which is your weakest? How can you develop your strength and strengthen your weakness?

3 Compare notes as a group to discover the strengths and weaknesses of your group.

4 Consider the key passage above. Why do
you think the disciples failed to
'see the harvest field'?
How might Jesus' comments on sowers and
reapers apply to being a world Christian?

THE ULTIMATE AUTHORITY

The Bible says a lot of things, but 'charity begins at home' isn't one of them! If we have any authority at all to take the message to our neighbours and the world, we will have to find it in the Bible. We are people under authority. We don't have the luxury of being able to 'make it up as we go along'. What we believe, and how we act, in areas such as sexuality, spiritual gifts and worship, should all flow out of an understanding of what the Bible says. Mission is in exactly the same position. If the Bible says nothing about it, let's stay at home, put our feet up and 'channel-surf' with our TV remote control!

On the other hand, if the Handbook does have something to say on the subject, we should find out what it is and then get on with doing what it says. Well, it does, and we should!

From the very beginning God demonstrates a commitment to help people get to know him and live together in peace and joy. Adam and Eve reject God's plan and have to face the consequence of separation from God and some hostility in their relationship with each other. God doesn't give up on them, or their family. He still wants a relationship with them, even though they have turned their backs on him. This scenario has been repeated millions of times in human history – and God's response has been consistent. His character of total goodness can't stand evil, but he goes on loving those who do evil, always wanting them to come back to him. His 'mission statement' has always included taking deliberate steps to go and look for people who are hiding from him, or who are looking for him, but have got lost. In the Garden of Eden he gets involved in the world's first ever game of hide and seek (Genesis 3:8–19)! Adam and Eve are found, then found out (Genesis 3:11f.), then thrown out (Genesis 3:23)! But God doesn't give up on them or their dependants; he is always looking for ways to draw them back into conversation and relationship. For example: Cain (4:13f.), Enoch (5:24); Noah (6:8).

And although it is soon obvious that a specific nation, the Jews, has been chosen as a channel of God's message, they are not to be the only ones who benefit. Throughout the Old Testament, Gentiles and Jews, the whole world, in fact, are the focus of God's search and rescue mission.

All the ends of the earth
    *will remember and turn to the L*ORD*,*
and all the families of the nations
    will bow down before him.
                        (Psalm 22:27)

In Isaiah 49:6 the Lord says:

'It is too small a thing for you to be my servant
    to restore the tribes of Jacob
    and bring those of Israel I have kept.
I will also make you a light for the Gentiles,
    that you may bring my salvation
        to the ends of the earth.'

It's pretty clear that our God wants everyone in every nation to be part of his family!

....

*'My name will be great among the nations, from the rising to the setting of the sun. In every place incense and pure offerings will be brought to my name, because my name will be great among the nations,' says the L*ORD *Almighty* (Malachi 1:11).

....

This missionary emphasis in the Godhead continued in the arrival of God's Son (whose mission statement was, 'For the Son of Man came to seek and to save what was lost'). His whole life, the death he died and the miracle of his resurrection – all were directed at pleasing his mission-minded Father (John 8:28–29).

....

'These early Christians (in the Book of Acts) were led by the Spirit to the main task of bringing people to God through Christ, and were not permitted to enjoy fascinating sidetracks.'

J. B. Philips

....

'There is no argument for missions. The total action of God in history, the whole revelation of God in Christ – this is the argument.'

James S. Stewart

....

'The Spirit of Christ is the spirit of missions, and the nearer we get to him the more intensely missionary we must become.'

Henry Martyn

....

'The Bible is a missionary book. Jesus Christ is the Father's missionary to a lost world.'

Harold Lindsell

....

God's will is that this mission-task is passed on to the church. God sent his Son and his Son sends us. When Jesus declared, 'Peace be with you! As the Father has sent me, I am sending you' (John 20:21), he makes this remarkable idea clear. We have the incredible privilege of sharing with the Father and the Son the job of going to the world with the good news. David Livingstone summed it up when he said, 'God had an only Son, and he was a missionary and a physician. A poor, poor imitation of Him I am, or wish to be.'

And it seems that the early church got the message. From Pentecost onward they saw their primary task as living in a new way and explaining this 'way' to all who would listen; three thousand responded on the day of Pentecost (Acts 2:41), another five thousand within a few weeks (Acts 4:4) and from then on there is a constant series of references to people responding to their missionary outreach (Acts 2:47; 5:14; 6:7 and so on). And this growth was not simply numerical. The missionary zeal of the early church pushed back the boundaries of gender, colour, race and nationality. This message was for everyone, this mission universal (Acts 1:8). In a thrilling series of raids on enemy territory, the gospel penetrated far beyond its early male, Jewish origins. The hated Samaritans (Acts 8:5), a black African (8:26f.), a religious bigot (9:1f.), a woman (9:36) and a Roman Centurion (10:1) – do these Christians have no discernment? They seem willing to take the gospel to anyone! Just like Jesus, the early church gets stuck in to feeding the hungry, looking after the poor and healing the sick. This mission, his mission, was their constant preoccupation. Acts 5:42 seems a pretty clear description of the working out of their own 'mission statement': 'Day after day, in the temple courts and from house to house, they never stopped teaching and proclaiming the good news that Jesus is the Christ!'

The two leading characters of the New Testament, Paul and Peter, demonstrate this mission enthusiasm in both their lives and letters: Peter, senior apostle and local evangelist; Paul, globe-trotting missionary statesman. Peter is captivated by a God who desperately longs for everyone to know him (2 Peter 3:9); even those who have conquered the Jews and now rule over them (c.f. Acts 10:1), unclean Gentiles (Acts 11:1–3)! Paul is converted and commissioned in an unmistakable encounter with Jesus in the suburbs of Damascus (Acts 9:15). And after years of church planting and evangelistic preaching, he still can't get over the wonder of a God who wants all of humanity, without distinction, to share this marvellous good news (Ephesians 3:6).

*'If a man goes overseas for any length of time we would
expect him to learn the language of the country to which
he is going. More than this is needed, however, if he is
really to communicate with the people among whom he
is living. He must learn another language – that of the
thought-forms of the people to whom he speaks. Only so
will he have real communication with them and to them.
So it is with the Christian church. Its responsibility is not
only to hold to the basic, scriptural principles of the
Christian faith, but to communicate these unchanging
truths "into" the generation in which it is living.*

*'Every generation of Christians has this problem of
learning how to speak meaningfully to its own age . . . If
we are to communicate the Christian faith effectively,
therefore, we must know and understand the thought
forms of our own generation. These will differ slightly
from place to place, and more so from nation to nation.'*

Francis Schaeffer, *Escape From Reason* (IVP, 1968).

So far we have discovered that God is mission-
orientated by nature and activity. So was his
Son, and so were the early church. The Bible is
shot through with this missionary spirit. But is it
merely a description of the way things were, or
is it a *prescription* for the way things ought to
be? What does the Bible have to say about the

role of individual Christians, and the church as a whole, today? The Bible affirms three principles which are vitally important in this area: a *continuing* mission, a *command* to mission, and a *climax* to mission.

A CONTINUING MISSION

Jesus is pretty clear that the missionary task will not end when he dies; in fact, this event will signal its beginning (John 20:19–23). The drawing of people to him was obviously going to take some time! Jesus anticipated that there would be believers he would never meet in the flesh, but as evangelism continued, converts would go on multiplying as his disciples made other disciples, and so on: 'My prayer is not for them alone. I pray also for those who will believe in me through their message' (John 17:20). Jesus assumed that some time would elapse between his death and resurrection, and his second coming. The period between his two appearances on our planet was to be taken up with missionary activity. When the whole world had heard, this would be the cue for his return to the world stage (Matthew 24:14). Christians in the late twentieth century are part of this 'between appearances' mission team.

A COMMAND TO MISSION

One of the very last things Jesus ever said was an instruction regarding the missionary task. Mark and Luke summarize this command (Mark 16:15; Luke 24:47–48), but perhaps the fullest account is in Matthew's Gospel (Matthew 28:18–20). 'Make disciples', commands Jesus. 'As you go about your business, wherever you travel in the nations of the world, baptise and teach.' Jesus is at pains to point out that this discipling responsibility will continue to the 'end of the age', so he promises that his presence will continue with them until the missionary task is completed. His command is to be fulfilled in the light of this comfort: 'I will be with you always.'

So the command (and the comfort!) are not time-limited. This is not a specific command to a particular group of first-century Jewish men! It is a command to disciples of Jesus in every age, to be obeyed until the final age dawns. The church has its marching orders from the commander-in-chief. Our role as individual believers may vary depending on our gifts and calling, but no disciple of Jesus can evade the thrust of his command. Only the King's return will remove the obligation of obeying the King's command!

And this command is just as relevant in our world of many religions as it has ever been. We must obey the command sensitively, with tact

41

and great respect for the followers of other religions. But we can't evade the truth that Jesus claimed: 'I am the way and the truth and the life. No-one comes to the Father except through me' (John 14:6). The command to evangelize is based on this fact.

THE CLIMAX OF MISSION

The Bible has a captivating view of the goal or climax of mission. It describes a future in which every language, people-group and country will be represented, altogether in a magnificent display of international co-operation and harmony (Revelation 7:9). The whole of history is moving towards this stupendous conclusion: a planet-wide worship and celebration event drawn from all the nations of the globe under the Lordship of Jesus. This event draws us into its fulfilment. As believers, we will be present; in mission we help others to be present. We are invited to participate in the destiny which God has prepared for all who love him. Corrie Ten Boom put it simply when she wrote,

> *When I enter that beautiful city*
> *And the saints all around me appear,*
> *I hope that someone will tell me,*
> *'It was you who invited me here'.*

Mission is the privilege we have of inviting others to share in this glorious future.

Sadly, the Bible also speaks of an alternative climax or destiny for the human race. Just as there is a heaven to be enjoyed, so there is a hell to be avoided. The Bible's teaching on judgment seems very harsh in these enlightened and tolerant times. But it is hard to get away from the fact that permanent separation from God will be the consequence of rejecting him (John 3:37; Mark 9:43f.; Matthew 25:41, 46).

. . . .

'All your life an unattainable ecstasy has hovered just beyond the grasp of your consciousness. The day is coming when you will wake to find, beyond all hope, that you have attained it, or else, that it was within your reach and you have lost it forever.'

C. S. Lewis, 'Heaven', in *The Problem of Pain* (Bles, 1945), p. 136.

. . . .

A strong motivation for mission is found in a full-blooded commitment to the Bible's teaching about the fate of those who refuse God's offer of love. Much of our personal evangelism and local church commitment to mission will be half-hearted until the awfulness of the destiny of the lost hits us. Too many of us are 'closet universalists' – surely it will all work out for everyone in the end? Unfortunately the Bible offers us no such assurance!

The Bible offers two destinies to the people of planet earth. Mission is the church's way of encouraging participation in the heavenly destiny and showing how the hellish destiny can be avoided. Either way, our destiny as believers compels us to invite other people to consider their own.

How can a God of love send people to hell?

Hell means total separation from everything good. The flames described in the Bible may be picture language, but the reality they represent is no figment of the imagination. One of the reasons it exists is because of the seriousness with which God takes the decisions of men and women. If we choose to reject him and his offer of life, with his way of escape from all the dirtiness in the world, he refuses to overrule our decision. He won't force us to accept his love, because that would rob us of the privilege of choice and make us mere robots. So we do have to take the consequences of our decisions. Which means by choosing to live without God we have indeed *chosen to live without God* – now and for ever. And it is no use asking why we can't choose to live without God in this life, but choose to live with him in the next. The question completely misses the point about the radical nature of the choice. It's as if we wanted to choose not to have any children of our own and then at the age of eighty to change our mind and want to have grown-up children around to look after us. It's too late; our earlier decision has had inevitable consequences. So it is with our decision about God. There comes a point (death) when our earlier decision is too far gone to change. Which means we have chosen to spend eternity living in the presence of our own sinfulness and in the absence of God.

All of this means that, far from God sending us to hell, we seem to be sending ourselves. After all, it would be most unreasonable to blame the doctor for our ill health if we refuse to take the medicine he prescribed! The divine doctor has diagnosed the sin-sickness of mankind and offered a forgiveness-cure. If we refuse or ignore the offer we will have to live with the disease. And that's what hell is: living after death with all our worst traits still raging inside us. But now they are unrestrained by God or social convention – a seething mass of unforgiven vices and unresolved conflicts. God does not want anyone to go to hell and so he has prepared a way for mankind to escape its horrors. He is in the business of getting people into heaven and not sending them to hell.

Stephen Gaukroger, *It Makes Sense* (Scripture Union, 1987).

So the Bible points us to the priority of mission with a relentless logic and a passionate enthusiasm. The nature and activity of God the Father, the work and words of God's Son and the example of the early church empowered by the Holy Spirit, are clear. The Holy Spirit goes on applying the Scripture to our lives as we bring ourselves under its authority. We are commanded to be activists in the cause of mission, right up to the return of Jesus, preparing for the great destiny which awaits us. Fundamentally, the Bible affirms that our Christian faith is a mission-faith; if it isn't we ought to question whether it is biblical faith at all!

CHAPTER TWO

THE ULTIMATE AUTHORITY

KEY PASSAGES

Matthew 25:41–46; 28:18–20; John 17:20

QUESTIONS FOR DISCUSSION

Review the sections in this chapter on 'A continuing mission'; 'A command to mission'; 'The climax of mission'.

Consider the Great Commission:

1 How do you suppose the eleven disciples felt on hearing these words of Jesus?

2 How do you feel about being part of Jesus' 'between appearances' mission team?

3 What do you think motivated the disciples to be obedient to the command?

4 What motivates you?

5 What things hinder you from full involvement in the team, and how can these hindrances be overcome?

6 In what ways are you currently involved in making other disciples?

7 How can you encourage one another in your group to be active members of this mission team?

chapter three

WHAT IS A MISSIONARY?

Is it a bird? Is it a plane? No! It's a missionary! For quite a large number of Christians even the word 'missionary' is a turn-off; no wonder so few ever think about becoming one. 'Missionary'. Pictures from our colonial past flash before our eyes: tea on a wooden verandah, fanned by an attractive, black house-boy; watching the sun set over the local water-hole; pith-helmets, khaki shorts and natives with bundles on their heads. Jokes about volunteering for a 'missionary position'! Isn't there something slightly eccentric about a 'missionary'?

This dreadful caricature is sometimes confirmed when you meet missionaries on leave in the West. They can appear out of touch in terms of dress, style of presentation and attitude. All this can give the impression that missionaries (and so mission) are out of date and out of touch. More street-crud rather than street-cred!

None of this is exactly designed to get you rushing to see your minister and offering your services in mission – here or overseas. For one thing, it would be bad for your image, and of course, there are other more 'attractive' things to be getting involved with. Despite all this, mission is incredibly important: it's a vital, biblical focus of the church of Jesus. And to do mission we obviously need people to do it – 'missionaries', or God's mission agents. Thousands of them, young and old, employed and unemployed, single and married, a whole army for God's kingdom purposes in the world.

I suppose changing the name might help, but to what? From 'missionary' to . . . gospel-truth transmitter? Operative with the spiritually challenged? There don't seem to be too many obvious alternatives. The use of 'international partner' is a recent attempt to emphasize that this work is often with and under the authority of a local, national leadership. Until we come up with a more acceptable name, it may be better to try and get a handle on what a missionary or a mission-motivated Christian actually does. What is this 'mission' they are engaged in?

Mission involves 'all that God sent his people in the world to do', to quote John Stott. This includes telling people about God in a way they can understand. It includes wanting people to have access to a local worshipping community and at least some of the Bible in their own language. It includes wanting hunger to be alleviated and disease to be minimized. It includes wanting freedom from torture, oppression and war. It includes wanting to make disciples of Jesus Christ. It includes wanting the whole world to receive the benefits of being part of the kingdom of God. It includes wanting God's will to be done on earth, as it is in heaven. This is mission.

The cross-cultural missionary

Definition: One who is commissioned and sent out by his or her local church to cross cultural boundaries in order to be a witness for Jesus Christ. These boundaries may be those of language, geography, or society.

He or she would also intentionally:

* introduce people to Christ by his or her life, attitudes, actions and words.

* seek to introduce those who come to Christ to join with others in the fellowship of a church. A church will need to be planted, if it doesn't exist!

In Ephesians 4:11–16, Paul clearly shows that our ascended Lord gave gifts of different kinds to people for different tasks within his kingdom. Not every Christian is a pastor or an apostle, an evangelist or a teacher. Similarly, we are not all called to be cross-cultural missionaries, in the sense described above. But we all are called to be involved in God's mission in one way or another. Some of us will cross the boundaries of society, geography and language. Others of us will provide support by our love, prayers, gifts and commitment.

To take a picture from the army – all Christians are under the command of Christ. We recognize that he is the supremo. We are committed to his purposes of reconciling everything to himself – things of earth and under heaven (Colossians 1:19–20). But some of us are commanded to be front-line personnel, going to places where the claims of Jesus are not yet recognized. In military terms, these could be the infantry, paratroops and marines. These front-liners would be backed up by the artillery, engineers, transport and support personnel. The front-line troops, however, also need the backup of logistics specialists, with their expertise in catering, administration, intelligence, and a host of other things, to maintain the front-line operation over long periods of time.

The enterprise of cross-cultural mission needs the resources and commitment of the whole body of the church, both in the 'sending' and 'receiving' countries. The cross-cultural missionary relies upon this vibrant web of support, and cannot function without it.

This sounds much more exciting than 'being a missionary', but it simply describes what true missionaries have always been about. They may have been working in Bolton or Buenos Aires, pastoring or planting crops, a mile from home or

5,000 miles from home. Everyone involved in God's mission is a witness.

And this witness can be described in three different, but complementary ways. It is about encountering, telling and demonstrating. Any one of these may be our primary personal calling as an agent of mission, but the mission task of the church involves all three elements.

ENCOUNTERING

The mission of Jesus was a mission where things happened! And some of these things were not your run-of-the-mill events. Blind eyes started seeing (John 9:25), leprosy patients got cured (Luke 17:11–14) and even dead people came back to life (John 11:43–44). What's more, those who had lives which had been invaded by evil – messing them up emotionally, mentally and spiritually – found Satan being unceremoniously kicked out (Luke 8:27–33).

The early church continued this tradition of seeing God move in power. Disabled beggars leapt to their feet (Acts 3:6–8), there was a miraculous jail-break (Acts 12:5–10) and the devil-inspired opposition was effectively silenced (Acts 13:9–11)!

The mission of the church involves a clash of two kingdoms – God's and Satan's. Our mission is to mount raids on Satan's kingdom, setting free his captives. This is warfare, and our weapons are not related to human ingenuity, but spiritual power. That is, mission is a super-natural activity. Neither the world, the flesh, nor the devil yields territory without a fight. A living encounter with Jesus is what serves these enemies of God with their eviction notice. Behind many social ills lie dark spiritual forces; behind political and social institutions which hinder the spread of the gospel, demonic agencies may be at work. This information is not designed to make us paranoid about the devil cropping up everywhere, but to remind us that he has already been disarmed (Colossians 2:15) and we should see that he is fully routed and put into retreat.

Mission which lacks this dimension of encoun-ter is not fully biblical. Many advances for the gospel in both 'telling' and 'demonstrating' have occurred when there has been clear evidence of God at work. Throughout church history there has been an awareness of God's power in mission; healing and deliverance from demons being particularly in evidence. In many parts of the world today mission workers tell of an oppressive atmosphere and of clear evidence of the devil in control of people's lives. I recently spoke with someone who had just returned from a remote part of North India. This person had come across children deliberately mutilated to aid in begging, baby girls murdered to avoid the expense of raising them, and an all-pervading, almost tangible sense of evil. In this kind of environment, spiritual authority is not a subject to be discussed, but a power to be exercised in order to survive.

In the West we are constantly reminded of evil at work here, in publicity like that surrounding the murder of O. J. Simpson's wife, and the trial of an English husband and wife involving the murder of many young people, including their own daughter, and allegations of sordid sexual abuse.

The tax collector in Torgau and the counsellor in Belgern have written to me to ask that I offer some good advice and help for Mrs John Korner's afflicted husband. I know of no worldly help to give. If the physicians are at a loss to find a remedy, you may be sure that it is not a case of ordinary melancholy. It must, rather, be an affliction that comes from the devil, and this must be counteracted by the power of Christ with the prayer of faith. This is what we do, and what we have been accustomed to do, for a cabinet maker here was similarly afflicted with madness and we cured him by prayer in Christ's name.

Accordingly you should proceed as follows: Go to him with a deacon and two or three good men.

Confident that you, as pastor of the place, are clothed with the authority of the ministerial office, lay your hands upon him and say, 'Peace be with you, dear brother, from God our Father and from our Lord Jesus Christ.' There upon repeat the Creed and the Lord's Prayer over him in a clear voice, and close with these words: 'O God, almighty Father, who hast told us through thy Son, "Verily, verily I say unto you, Whatsoever ye shall ask the Father in my name, he will give it to you"; who hast commanded and encouraged us to pray in his name, "Ask, and ye shall receive", and who in like manner hast said, "Call upon me in the day of trouble: I will deliver thee, and thou shalt glorify me"; we unworthy sinners, relying on these thy words and commands, pray for thy mercy with such faith as we can muster. Graciously deign to free this man from all evil, and put to nought the work that Satan has done in him, to the honour of thy name and the strengthening of the faith of believers; through the same Jesus Christ, thy Son, our Lord, who liveth and reigneth with thee, world without end. Amen.' Then, when you depart, lay your hands upon the man again and say, 'These signs shall follow them that believe; they shall lay hands on the sick, and they shall recover.'

Martin Luther

TELLING

People everywhere need to hear the good news explained to them in ways they can understand. Romans 10:13–14 highlights the importance of this! 'Everyone who calls on the name of the Lord will be saved. How, then, can they call on the one they have not believed in? And how can they believe in the one of whom they have not heard? And how can they hear without some- one preaching to them?' There is simply no substitute for preaching the truth – to indivi- duals or a huge crowd – explaining the basic facts of the gospel and calling for a response. Of course, this must be done sensitively, humbly and in a way which is culturally appropriate. We will want to take great care to avoid unneces- sary offence by our tone, dress, use of illustra- tions and style of presentation. Whether we are preaching in a pub in England or a market-place in India we will always want to treat our hearers with respect. We will plan to avoid manipulative techniques and tricks or gimmicks which will trivialize our message. Certainly we must act in these wise ways . . . but we must act! Sometimes we have become so sophisticated, so 'careful' that the simple power of the gospel is all but extinguished. The roar of the Lion of Judah has become the muted miaow of a castrated tom cat!

The good news desperately needs telling! Millions are going to an eternity without God. Who will tell them of God's amazing love for them, his longing to see them set free from wrong, filled with his love and power, guaranteed a relationship with him for ever? How can they find out about all this if no-one tells them?

Sometimes this can be the hardest and most easily forgotten part of mission. Lots of countries which accept doctors or agriculturalists who are Christians, would not dream of letting an evangelist or pastor into their territory. This means that 'telling' has to be done discretely and cautiously; there is often great pressure on missionaries for it not to happen at all. Even in the West we know what a struggle it is to get beyond friendship evangelism to articulating the gospel. Some of us have had non-Christian friends, family or neighbours for years, and they have never heard us describe our Christian faith. We had hoped our Christian lifestyle would prompt them to ask questions, but they seem remarkably un-curious! And, of course, we don't want to be 'pushy' and embarrass them, or us, so we say nothing. Sometimes it is a case of our silence being yellow not golden!

Mission involves verbal communication. We have a message to pass on to the world which people need to hear, understand and respond to. This message involves concepts such as repentance, faith and forgiveness. It demands a response to its statements of truth. The words of an African enquirer in the first century sum up the cry of a needy world today!

....

> *The Spirit told Philip, 'Go to that chariot and stay near it.' Then Philip ran up to the chariot and heard the man reading Isaiah the prophet. 'Do you understand what you are reading?' Philip asked. 'How can I,' he said, 'unless someone explains it to me?' So he invited Philip to come up and sit with him* (Acts 8:29–31).

....

Philip tells the African leader about Jesus and he responds with faith, asking for baptism. Telling has helped this individual to move from enquiring to deciding.

DEMONSTRATING

The Bible consistently describes mission in terms of compassion as well as communication, that is, by works as well as words. The Old Testament encouraged acts of kindness, particularly to the poor, famished and homeless (Isaiah 58:7). Jesus spent a lot of time meeting people's physical needs: healing the sick (*e.g.* Luke 8:48), feeding the hungry (*e.g.* Luke 9:16–17), even rescuing frightened fishermen on a stormy lake (Mark 4:38–39).

Jesus also made it clear that these practical demonstrations of God's love were to be continued by the church (*e.g.* Matthew 25:31f.), not as an optional extra but as an integral part of the missionary task. 'Demonstrations' of the good news are neither more inferior expressions of mission than 'telling', nor are they replacements for 'telling' – they are partners in the mission!

The need for these practical acts of care is obvious everywhere in our hurting world. Our television screens and newspapers bombard us with the latest images of famine, earthquake and flood. In the towns and cities of our own western countries, the homeless sleep rough, debt cripples thousands of families, and children are abused and neglected. Jesus hears the cry of the hurting and our mission is to respond in love. These are people for whom Christ died, people Jesus loves. He wants to use the church to answer their anguished prayers for help. They can't eat a portion of scripture nor live in a sermon! Compassion demands a different response.

In the UK alone . . .

30,000 children and young people were added to
the Child Protection Register in 1994.

Care for the Family

A fifth of Europe's poor live in the UK.

Study by David Budge and Antony Dore, *Times Educational
Supplement*, 3 March 1995.

There were 3.3 million county court summonses for debt in
1991, an increase of 61% on 1988.

The National Association of Citizens Advice Bureaux.

1 in 5 families are headed by a lone parent.
2 in 3 lone parent families live below the poverty line.
1 in 5 households is in debt.
70% of separating couples cite money as the prime reason.
1,000 people become homeless daily.
2 in 3 homeless households include children.

Evangelical Alliance

The number of people claiming income support rose to a
record 5.6 million last year, up more than 500,000
on the previous year.

DSS figures quoted in *The Daily Telegraph*, 26 August 1994.

These 'good deeds' which demonstrate God's love, often open up opportunities for 'telling' which otherwise would have fallen on deaf ears. Christian action can prepare the way for Christian preaching. But we must be careful not to be manipulative. These 'demonstrations' are to be done because they are part of mission, part of acting on the way God feels about our broken world; not simply as a lever to make people more responsive to evangelism.

. . . .

'Jesus was not afraid to look human need in the face, in all its ugly reality. And what he saw invariably moved him to compassion, and so to compassionate service. Sometimes, he spoke. But his compassion never dissipated itself in words; it found expression in deeds. He saw, he felt, he acted. The movement was from the eye to the heart, and from the heart to the hand. His compassion was always aroused by the sight of need, and it always led to constructive action.
It seems incontrovertible that if we are even to begin to follow the real Jesus, and to walk in his shoes, we must seize every opportunity to "do good". Our good works will show the genuineness of our love, and our love will show the genuineness of our faith.'

John R. W. Stott

. . . .

Many non-Christians in the past have 'converted' as a way of keeping the practical support going! Their faith lasts as long as the money continues. We must not encourage this kind of response by attaching 'strings' to our care. The hungry must be fed, whether or not they turn to Christ. Of course we long for them to know him, but care is an action which needs no 'spiritual' justification.

So being a partner in mission means being part of God's mission to his world. This mission, for which the whole church bears responsibility, involves 'encountering', 'telling' and 'demonstrating' the gospel. Only this 'whole' gospel has a hope of reaching the whole world.

WHAT IS A MISSIONARY?

KEY PASSAGES

John 17:11–23; Romans 10:13–14.

QUESTIONS FOR DISCUSSION

'Everyone involved in God's mission is a witness. And this witness can be described in three different, but complementary ways. It is about encountering, telling and demonstrating' (p. 53).

1 Encountering, telling and demonstrating. In which of these areas do you personally have the most experience?

2 Are there any in which you have no experience? What first steps can you make in that area?

3 Most western Christians have fears when it comes to speaking to others about Christ. What specifically are we afraid of? What scriptures can you bring to bear on these fears?

4 What one step will you take this week to face one of your fears and overcome it? How can the group support you in this?

5 Which do you think is easier and why: to 'tell' the gospel message to people in your own country or to go to another culture to 'tell'?

REPENT

WHO WILL GO?

....

'Woe to me!' I cried. 'I am ruined! For I am a man of unclean lips, and I live among a people of unclean lips, and my eyes have seen the King, the LORD Almighty.'
Then one of the seraphs flew to me with a live coal in his hand, which he had taken with tongs from the altar. With it he touched my mouth and said, 'See, this has touched your lips; your guilt is taken away and your sin atoned for.'
Then I heard the voice of the Lord saying, 'Whom shall I send? And who will go for us?'
And I said, 'Here am I. Send me!' (Isaiah 6:5–8).

....

God's mission needs people who will go. Men and women who have heard his call and respond with obedience. Not super-heroes who leap over all obstacles with a single bound. Not mega-saints who have never had an ungodly thought in their lives. Not spiritual giants who have already memorized the entire Old Testament. God's mission needs ordinary men and women who want to do what God wants them to do, above everything else. This means *you* or me, or the person in the seat next to me in church. Yes, 'It could be you'; not a winner of the National Lottery, but a mission agent for God!

Of course, while everyone is called to be a partner in mission, not everyone is called to be a missionary (see p. 53). Years ago an Admiral Foote was visiting Siam (now Thailand) and had invited the King and members of the royal court to a dinner on his ship. Before the meal was served, he prayed, asking God to bless the food. When he had finished, the King of Siam said that he thought only missionaries prayed before eating a meal. To which the admiral replied, 'Yes, but every Christian is a missionary!'

Every Christian is called to be a missionary in the sense that we are witnesses to what God has done in our lives, and wherever we go we must be his messengers, through holy lives and spoken witness. Not everyone is called to dedicate their lives to 'full-time Christian service' either here or overseas. But many are called to be God's mission agents in the world of banking, education, medicine, management, civil service or business. It is vital to have lots of 'salty'

Christians who are bringing up families, serving in shops, policing the streets or building our homes. Every member of every church must fulfil his or her mission responsibilities in the area God has placed him or her. The call to Marks and Spencer is just as significant as the call to Africa! The crucial thing is to be a partner in mission wherever we are.

But in addition to this call on every Christian, some are called to exercise their gifts in specifically 'Christian' activity – either in one's country Kingdom or abroad – through a church or mission agency. And the need is great for dedicated missionaries of this kind, and particularly for those who will go to another culture, country or language group. Of all 'full-time Christian workers', about 90% work with the privileged western world and only 10% work with the 90% of the population in the rest of the world!

What causes this reluctance to serve in full-time mission? There seems to be a number of factors. For example:

* Materialism has gripped the church as well as the world. There is a reluctance to accept a lower standard of living, which is often the consequence of working abroad.

* Mission abroad has a slightly dated, old-fashioned image. Long-term service with an established missionary agency can seem far less glamorous than many other ministry options.

* We live in an instant-results society. There is often great resistance to the years of language training and cultural orientation. We want to serve God *now*!

* The world we live in values tolerance above truth. There is an undercurrent of feeling in some churches that we have no right to interfere in the affairs of other countries. This is, to some extent, a reaction to our western colonial past. It leaves even the most fervent believer wondering if local Christians should be left to get on with the job in their own countries.

No wonder mobilizing the church to release this kind of missionary is extremely difficult. Yet the need is so great. Over 3,000 languages are without the Scriptures and almost 200 major languages have not yet received the Christian message on the radio. About 40% of the world's population have never heard the gospel in a way they can understand, yet many of us hear it several times a week. Can it be right that some have heard the message hundreds of times when there are millions who have never heard it once?

More than ever we need women and men to

respond to the great challenge of world mission. It will be costly in terms of family, health and comfort. It will demand dying to self and living for him – not in theory but in cold, hard practice. When James Calvert sailed as a missionary to the cannibals of the Fiji Islands, the captain of the ship urged him not to go ashore: 'You will lose your life and the lives of those with you if you go among such savages.' Calvert replied, 'We died before we came here.' In 1839 John Williams, with his wife, went to the cannibals of New Hebrides in the South Pacific. After a short period of service there they were both clubbed to death. Eighteen years later, in 1857, G. N. Gordon and his wife went to the islands, only to be murdered in 1861. John Paton followed a few years later and the first communion service, with twelve converts, was held in 1869. This kind of courage and commitment is needed among us today. Cannibals may be rarer, but the cost of missionary service can still be very high.

It is very important not to minimize the personal cost of missionary obedience. In human terms it can be a risky decision with the potential to affect adversely family, career, comfort and health. An advert which appeared some years ago sums it up:

....

Ability to mix with people, mix concrete, wade rivers, write articles, love one's neighbour, deliver babies, sit cross-legged, drain swamps, digest questionable food, patch human weakness, suffer fools gladly and burn the midnight oil – these are required for service!

Persons allergic to ants, babies, beggars, chop suey, cockroaches, curried crabs, duplicators, guitars, humidity, indifference, itches, jungles, mildew, minority groups, mud, poverty, sweat and unmarried mothers had better think twice before applying!

....

Who will take up this challenge? Will you go as God calls? You may not think you are holy enough, old enough, young enough, clever enough, healthy enough, wise enough or even bothered enough – but are you willing enough?

And don't be fooled into believing some of the common myths about missionaries.

Common myths

Myth 1: Missionaries always have a dramatic 'call'!
No they don't! Moses did and so did the apostle Paul (Exodus 3 and Act 9), but lots of missionaries simply had a gradual and growing conviction that God wanted them to serve in this way.

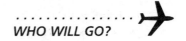
Perhaps we should be ready to go unless we are sure God has called us to stay!

Myth 2: Missionaries never shout at their kids!
Of course this is true . . . and so is the fact that Norway always wins the Eurovision Song Contest, the Pope is a Jehovah's Witness and Truro is about to win football's Premier Division! Missionaries have all the struggles associated with being a human and a Christian. Perfection is not a requirement.

Myth 3: Missionaries are naturally adventurous!
Usually the rugged types, they enjoy poor sanitation, consider large spiders their friends and would give anything to experience malaria! In reality, the opposite is often the case. God gives courage as the need arises, not normally in advance. Throughout church history God has used many weak and frail people in some of the toughest situations. Note: there may be a biblical principle here: see 2 Corinthians 12:9–10!

Myth 4: Missionaries are good at public speaking!
Many agricultural, medical and administrative missionaries don't have this gift. (Nor do some of the preachers!) Most people improve in this area with practice, but for many mission workers it is not a major component of what they do.

Most of the basic qualifications for missionary service abroad or far afield are related to character. (In the next chapter we will look at some of the practical steps and training required.) Humility, patience and the ability to control your temper may be as valuable to you in God's service as a knowledge of New Testament Greek or a thorough grasp of missiology.

On one occasion a mission agency decided to test an applicant's character in an unusual way. At 3.00 a.m. on a cold morning a candidate walked into the office for a scheduled interview with the candidate's secretary of a missionary society. He waited until 8.00 a.m. when the interviewer arrived! The interviewer said, 'First, spell Baker.' 'B-A-K-E-R,' the young man said. 'Very good. Now let's see what you know about figures. How much is two times two?' 'Four,' replied the applicant. 'Very good,' the interviewer said. 'I'll recommend to the society that you be appointed. You have passed the test.'

At the Council meeting the candidate's secretary spoke highly of the applicant and said, 'He has all the qualifications of a missionary. Let me explain. First, I tested him on self-denial. I told him to be at my office at three in the morning. He left a warm bed and came out in the cold without a word of complaint. Second, I tried him out on punctuality. He appeared on time. Third, I examined him on patience. I made him

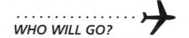

wait five hours to see me. Fourth, I tested him on temper. He failed to show any sign of it; he didn't even question my delay. Fifth, I tried his humility. I asked him questions that a small child could answer, and he showed no offence. He meets the requirements and will make the missionary we need.'

Hudson Taylor's qualifications for a missionary

* A life yielded to God and controlled by his Spirit.

* A restful trust in God for the supply of all needs.

* A sympathetic spirit and a willingness to take a lowly place.

* Tact in dealing with men and adaptability toward circumstances.

* Zeal in service and steadfastness in discouragement.

* Love for communion with God and for the study of his Word.

* Some experience and blessing in the Lord's work at home.

* A healthy body and a vigorous mind.

So, will you go? Go next door or to the office of a colleague down the hall? Go across town or across the world? Go to a relative, a friend or a total stranger? 'How long will you waver between two opinions? If the LORD is God, follow him' (1 Kings 18:21).

There's a beach in Jacksonville, Florida, which has lifeguards stationed on it because of a strong, but unseen, undertow. Many times a week they dive into the water to rescue someone who appears to be getting into difficulties. Sometimes the swimmer would have managed without help, sometimes a life is saved or serious injury prevented. In the lifeguard station a huge motto in red letters hangs on the wall – their 'mission statement'. It reads, *'If in doubt, go!'* Perhaps this should be on the wall of every church building and certainly etched onto the heart of every church member.

John Mott, a missionary statesman, gave his whole life to enthusing the church about mission. His first official international involvement came when he was twenty-three years old and this continued in various ways until he was well into his eighties! At the close of an address urging people to prioritize world evangelism on their personal agenda, he concludes: 'In view of the constraining memories of the cross of Christ and the love with which he has loved us, let us rise and resolve, at whatever cost of self denial,

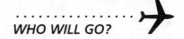

that live or die, we shall live or die for the evangelisation of the world in our day.'

Will we go in our day, as he did in his?

CHAPTER FOUR

WHO WILL GO?

KEY PASSAGES

Isaiah 6:1–8; Jeremiah 1:4–10.

QUESTIONS FOR DISCUSSION

1 Both Isaiah and Jeremiah felt inadequate in the face of God's call. What enabled them to fulfil their call? In what ways do you identify with them?

2 As a group, identify as many things as you can that all Christians are 'called' to. Which of these relate to taking the good news about Jesus to others?

3 On page 72 we read: 'Who will take up this challenge . . . are you willing enough?' Is being willing to go enough? Why/why not?

4 Hudson Taylor's list (p. 75) and 2 Corinthians 12:9–10 might suggest that most, if not all, Christians could be missionaries. Do you agree with this? Why/why not?

READY TO GO?

. . . .

Ann Judson, a pioneer missionary to Burma, once wrote about what qualifications were needed by missionaries.

'In encouraging young people to come out as missionaries, do use the greatest caution. One wrong-minded, obstinate person would ruin us. Humble, quiet, persevering folk of sound, sterling character, with good accomplishment and some natural aptitude to acquire a language; people with an amiable, yielding temper, willing to take the lowest place; who live close to God and who are willing to suffer all things for Christ's sake without being proud of it – these are the kind of people we need.'

. . . .

If you have been convinced that you should go, what is the next step? Quite a few people are challenged by a missionary speaker, at a conference or even by a book like this! But that's as far as it goes. Emotions of the heart must result in enquiry of the mind and activity of the body! If your mission is not to be employed 'full-time' by a local church or Christian organization, this chapter is still for you!

GROWING

As you go, grow. Work hard to ensure that you have the basics of Christian discipleship in place. Good foundations are essential in our lives as we think about building something of God into other people's. It's good to have a basic under-standing of the structure and general content of the Bible books. A simple grasp on what the Bible teaches about prayer, salvation, assurance, guidance, the church and evangelism, is a good foundation for whatever God may guide you to in the future.

Consider doing a discipleship course with a friend or a correspondence course with a Bible College. You could ask one of your church leaders for help or visit a Christian bookshop where they will be able to advise you. Even if you have been a Christian for years, a refresher course in these areas would be a good idea.

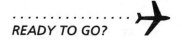
THINKING

What is God calling you to do? If you feel you may be being called to specific missionary employment, some of these next suggestions will be particularly appropriate. All who are concerned about missions will find them helpful to consider, however.

My first suggestion is to think and pray about what God may be calling you to. There are some attitudes to Christian service which are unhelpful. 'Full-time' Christian work is not somehow superior to secular work. Missionaries and pastors are not God's special favourites. I.B.M. is as much a mission field as Asia! But the opposite attitude is also wrong. 'Full-time' service need not be an escape into a religious ghetto or a retreat for weak people from the pressures of the world. Just because it is for some, does not mean it is for everybody. (Even some of my non-Christian friends still wonder when I'm going to get a 'proper job'!)

World mission is the responsibility of every believer, but we will not all fulfil our responsibility in the same way. Careful thought must be given to how and where we are to be God's mission agents – our obedience is the important thing. We are in the right place, doing the right thing, when we are doing God's thing in God's place!

. . . .

One day Mr Wilfred Grenfell, medical missionary to Labrador, was guest at a dinner in London together with a number of socially prominent British men and women. During the course of the dinner, the lady seated next to him turned and said, 'Is it true, Dr Grenfell, that you are a missionary?' Dr Grenfell looked at her for a moment before replying, 'Is it true, madam, that you are not?'

. . . .

EXPLORING

There are quite a few things you can do to begin to explore what God might be calling you to. You could start by having a conversation with your minister or other church leaders. Listen carefully to what they say. They often have a more objective view of our character and gifts which it is helpful to hear (though perhaps not always enjoyable!). Don't be discouraged if they appear slightly negative about your desire to serve God. Remember how many similar conversations they may have had which did not result in any action. Any less-than-enthusiastic response may simply be out of a concern to see how serious you really are about all this.

It is vital to check out any sense of call with a responsible church leader. Some people can be

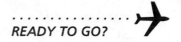
Short-term work

Application form
Name
Address
Date of birth
Marital status
Describe your educational background and academic qualifications.
List your previous employers and work experience.
How did you become a Christian?
What church do you attend?
What Christian work have you been involved in?
How would you describe your state of health?
Provide two references (one from the minister of your church) in support of your application.

This is a summary of half a dozen application forms from specific Christian organizations. If you are applying for long-term service the questions would be more extensive and more detailed (see the sample on p. 154 at end of this book for an example). If you are going to work with children you would also be asked questions about any criminal convictions you have had and whether or not you are willing to be checked by the police.

You would usually be asked to supply a couple of passport size photographs of yourself.

extremely certain about their call – but wrong! Some are very uncertain and need help in clarifying things. We need the wisdom and maturity of others.

It can also be valuable to talk to a missionary who is home on leave, or fax or phone a mission worker abroad to find out how they became convinced about Christian service in this way. It is sometimes worth interviewing a vicar or pastor in your area who is from another denomination than your own. Different traditions see the call to service in different ways and it can be useful to be exposed to other approaches.

Why not begin to subscribe to a couple of missionary magazines; one dealing with work at home and one with work abroad. (See the resource section at the end of the book.) Do they describe something which you could contribute to or would enjoy? As you pray about what you read, God may show you possible future roles.

WORKING

Going abroad is unlikely to turn you into a Christian worker! 'Work where you are, so you can work where you're sent' is a good motto. Another is, 'If you won't be missed, don't go!' Being a loyal church member and a faithful participant in local church life is vitally important.

Short-term mission

Pros and cons

Pros

1. Gives vision of the need in other countries.
2. Requires no expensive language study.
3. No need to bring much luggage, no removal expenses.
4. Can witness to those who speak English, or through an interpreter.
5. No family who has to travel with you.
6. No long-term investment – if you fall ill, you can be sent home.
7. Opportunity to test call.
8. Effective in restricted countries, *e.g.* Turkey or Iran.
9. Generates interest in home churches.
10. Many short-termers come back as long-termers.
11. Many become lifelong supporters of missions.

Cons

1. Inexperience. No gradual introduction possible.
2. No language (cannot answer telephone or read timetable).
3. Clueless about culture even when interpreted.
4. No time to build long-term relationships for evangelism.
5. No time to plant churches.
6. Short-term projects may siphon off funds from long-term ones.
7. Distraction for long-termers asked for assistance.

Summary

Short-term work is very useful for the participants in gaining a vision of the great need of the world for the gospel.

Michael Griffiths, *Tinker, Tailor, Missionary?* (IVP, 1992), p. 127.

'Lone rangers' rarely last long. Committed participation in the local body of Christ will enable spiritual development and might help ensure that you don't make big mistakes on your exploration of God's will. Your minister will be able to write you a good reference for a missionary society if he has already seen you at work in his church!

And there are other areas of Christian work you can explore as you test the waters of God's call. Some missionary societies offer opportunities to do short-term work (anything from two weeks to two years) in countries where they operate. To do this you may be able to take time off work, use part of your vacation or put to use a period between jobs. People taking early retirement may have a huge amount to contribute. In the UK, for example, there are beach missions, holiday clubs and evangelism teams which provide great opportunities, mainly in the summer. Quite a few organizations arrange these activities, and will send you their literature (see the list at the back of the book).

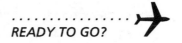
Pros and cons of being a 'tentmaker'

Countries with no restrictions on entry allow two options: full-time missionary or professional overseas 'tentmaker'.

Full-time missionary
Pros
1. Allows full-time activity as evangelist and church-planter.
2. Allows setting aside adequate time for language learning.
3. Allows close integration with national church.
4. Suited to those who can do one thing well at a time.
Cons
1. May be despised as a religious professional.
2. Is barred from entering some countries.
3. Approach to others is seen to have a religious motive.

Professional overseas 'tentmaker'
Pros
1. Attracts respect as making a secular contribution.
2. May reach 'high level' people socially.
3. Can witness through daily work.
4. Costs nothing to the sending church.
5. May be generously salaried and therefore able to support Christian work on the spot from personal income.
Cons
1. May never achieve skills in foreign language.
2. May be isolated in expatriate ghetto.
3. May have to join segregated expatriate church.
4. Has only limited time for church work.
5. Requires higher spiritual gifts than a full-timer.

Countries with no entry or visas for missionaries allow one option: part-time 'tentmaker'.

Part-time 'tentmaker'

This Christian is admitted because of professional skills in medicine, teaching, business or diplomacy. He or she witnesses by the quality of his or her daily work, by taking opportunities in the course of it, and in free time: sometimes under restrictions not to 'proselytize'. It demands probably a higher measure of spiritual gift than a professional missionary, because of the limited time available. And at the home end, it requires at least as much moral and prayer support.

M. Griffiths, *Tinker, Tailor, Missionary?* (IVP, 1992), pp. 69–70.

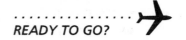
MATURING

Being part of a Christian organization or church staff is not always as easy as it might appear. Any image you have of sitting around all day singing choruses, studying Bible passages and having lots of fellowship time, should be erased from your mind! Just like any other workplace, you could encounter bad temper, gossip and fragile egos. It takes real maturity not to become cynical when you work with God's people! Good relationship skills are very important in the task of mission. You may be called on to relate to mission workers from other countries, national Christians and church leaders, and the non-Christian residents of the area you are working in; all in the 'pressure cooker' atmosphere of unfamiliar cuisine, culture, customs and climate. Add to this the fact that you are not feeling too well, are tired and homesick. Will you have the maturity to be a calm, positive influence in such an environment? I accept that even the archangel Gabriel might fail this particular test, but the principle is important. Emotional maturity is an important feature of successful, long lasting survival in the task of mission.

Another important aspect of maturity is discipline. Discipline in our use of time and money in particular. Christian workers often have to take a great deal of personal responsibility for setting their own work schedule. Either of the opposite evils of laziness and work-obsession will not serve you well in Christian service. At one end of the spectrum you will kill God's work and at the other end it will kill you! Our use of money can reveal worrying personality traits. Embrace generosity but avoid waste; and of course scrupulous honesty in financial matters is essential.

Maturity in sexual relationships is another crucial area. Sexual indiscretion is, sadly, too common among Christian workers. This, of course, discredits the gospel and damages both the people and the agency for which they work. Coming to terms with your own sexuality is a necessary facet of preparation for mission work.

All this talk about maturity could drive you to despair. Maturity, after all, can't be studied for or discovered at a conference! The important thing is *movement* towards maturity. We can reflect prayerfully on our life's experiences and make progress in maturity: *becoming* more self-aware, *becoming* more aware of how we affect others, *becoming* more disciplined, and so on. This process can be strengthened by having an honest friend who will tell us the truth in love. A prayer partner, a spiritual director or a discipler could all fulfil this kind of role.

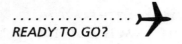
....

'So far in the history of the world there have never been enough mature people in the right places.'

George B. Chisholm

....

'Mature people are made not out of good times but out of bad times.'

Hyman Judah Schachtel

....

'The discipline of desire is the background of character.'

John Locke

....

'One of the marks of a mature person is the ability to dissent without creating dissension .'

Don Robinson

....

'Maturity begins to grow when you can sense your concern for others outweighing your concern for yourself.'

John MacNaughton

....

LEARNING

You can't become a brain surgeon overnight! Training and experience are essential. Whatever skills you bring to Christian work, additional training is almost always appropriate.

It can be useful to read some Christian biographies, but do make sure you read accounts of missionaries from the last twenty years, such as Jackie Pullinger, Chet Bitterman or Thomas Hale, as well as from the last two centuries. If a book paints a picture of a Christian hero with no flaws and portrays a story of uninterrupted success – get another book!

It is important to learn more about the area you feel God may be calling you to. We are all called to the 'world' so we ought to take steps to learn more about the way it works. Read a newspaper and perhaps a news magazine; keep abreast of world news as well as national-interest stories. If you feel called, for example, to work among young people, begin to ask questions about what influences and motivates them. Look at the magazines they read, listen to their music, interview a teacher, even talk to a teenager! If you feel called to a specific country or continent, find out about its population-mix, politics, geography, church life and culture. Most good libraries will provide material on this and some excellent material is available in

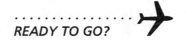
Patrick Johnstone's, *Operation World* (O. M. Publishing, 1993).

Features of the western world

* Objective truth is replaced by the view that we have to construct our own truths (relativism).

* Blurring of distinctions: such as right and wrong, people and machines, people and animals, male and female, the real world and virtual reality, fantasy and reality, God and nature.

* Search for the transcendent. The magical, mysterious and mystical offer a powerful attraction.

* Nature becomes sacred Mother Nature. A new paganism is establishing itself.

* Loss of hope and idealism. People no longer look optimistically to the future. Nostalgia is evident (in popular music and fashion, for example).

If you get involved in a short-term project (say, for a few weeks) the agency you have applied to will provide some kind of orientation or training. Once you get involved in a commitment to a longer-term period of service, the training requirement will be more extensive. You may be asked to undergo a period of theological education as well as language and 'culture-shock' preparation. Be prepared to spend years, rather than months getting ready for some types of missionary work.

And, of course, it is best to plan on a lifetime of learning and training. The best Christian workers are always trying to enhance their skills and develop their understanding. Sabbaticals, study leave, conferences and keeping up to date with your reading are all features of a mission worker who wants to make a significant long-term contribution to their area of work.

_____

Some worldwide trends

* *Economic*. Increase in economic disparity and other injustices between rich and poor – within nations and between nations.

* *Social and political*. Two major forces are more and more in conflict. These are unification and fragmentation. Technology and the media mainly contribute to an increasing standardization of lifestyle throughout the world. At the same time, there is an increase in nationalism, ethnic awareness, minority group solidarity and individualism.

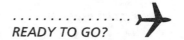

* *Population.* There is a dramatic shift to urban dwelling throughout the world, with a subsequent rise in mega cities. In many parts of the world the majority of the population are children or young people. The family is disintegrating under pressures of modern change as well as because of moral decline.

* *Environmental.* Modern social change in lifestyle is resulting in an environmental crisis unprecedented in history. Our grandchildren and great-grandchildren may accuse twentieth-century people of being 'ecological criminals'.

* *Religions.* World religions are in revival, and cults are on the increase as we approach the end of the millennium. Within the Christian church there has been a shift in the centre of gravity from the West to the 'two-thirds' world in church growth.

PRAYING

....

'God's acquaintance is not made hurriedly. He does not bestow His gifts on the casual, or hasty comer or goer. To be much alone with God is the secret of knowing Him and of influence with Him.'

E. M. Bounds

....

Prayer is an indispensable part of the preparation for a life of service. Through prayer God can confirm, for example, what part of the world you should serve him in and what you should be doing when you get there.

Regular conversations with God make us familiar with his voice and therefore more sensitive to his direction.

Without the 'listening to God', many of us are prone to rush headlong into the wrong thing. People with different personalities see the fruit of inadequate prayer in an almost permanent indecision. China? Africa? Manchester? Their final location changes weekly, on the basis of the last missionary speaker they heard or the last missionary biography they read! A sermon on being salt and light at work convinces them to get a 'normal' job at the bank; a TV documentary on African hunger sends them scurrying to get an application form from Tear Fund!

Faithful prayer, patient waiting on God, can give us a quiet, growing certainty about the call of God on our lives. Good decisions flow best when God has been allowed, in a paraphrase of a well-known hymn, to 'drop his still dews of quietness, till all our strivings cease; taking from our souls the strain and stress, until our ordered lives confess the beauty of His peace!'

The Top Ten

The Top Ten sending countries of the non-western world in 1988 were as follows (the numbers indicate active missionaries):
India: 8,905
Nigeria: 2,595
Zaire: 2,731
Burma: 2,560
Kenya: 2,242
Brazil: 2,040
Philippines: 1,814
Ghana: 1,545
Zimbabwe: 1,540
Korea: 1,184

Source: Robin Thomson, *World Christian*
(Lynx/St John's Extension Studies, 1992).

But prayer is vital for an equally important reason. God not only wants to tell us where to go and what to do, but how to *be*! That is, God is more concerned about our character than he is about our career. From his point of view, our geographical location and specific job description are less important than the Christlikeness of our lives. Prayerful, Jesus-centred people can make an impact for God almost anywhere; prayerless people do mess things up for God almost everywhere!

The modern story of world mission

The modern story began in the nineteenth century. Here are just a few examples.

* *Burma and Thailand*. Back in 1833, the Karens of Burma, who had only recently been evangelized, began outreach to the Kachin, a very different people, as well as to other Karens in Thailand. The Burma Baptist Convention is still the largest single missionary agency in Asia.

* *Tongans* planted the church in Fiji in 1835. Their king sent a message to the paramount chief of Fiji, preparing the way for a group of Tongan missionaries! British missionaries joined the partnership later in the same year. Well over 1,000 missionaries have been sent between the many islands of the Pacific since then, many travelling from island to island in their deep-sea canoes.

* *Jamaicans* began missionary work in Cameroon in 1893. They started Bible translation, printing and education. Today Caribbean Christians from Britain continue to work in Ghana, Nigeria, Liberia and other West African countries.

* *Latin American* countries have been sending missionaries within their continent, as well as to Spain, Portugal and the USA. COMIBAM, a congress on mission in Sâo Paulo in 1987, gave a new push to send missionaries outside the continent. There is a special interest in working in the Muslim countries

of North Africa and the Middle East.
A Brazilian girl heard about Asians from Hindu and Muslim
backgrounds. She came to London to learn English and is
now working with Asians in Manchester.

* *India*. India's missionary movement goes back to 1884,
when the Methodist Church sent a missionary to Singapore.
The Indian Missionary Society was founded in 1903, followed
soon after by the National Missionary Society. Both are still
active. But the explosion of missionary growth began in the
fifties and sixties. Individuals, churches and small groups
began to go, or dream about going, to unreached areas of
north India. 'Go or Send' was the motto of one of the
groups. Today their efforts have grown into thousands of
cross-cultural workers all over India, and abroad as well. A
marine biologist from Madras left his research to work with
students in Thailand. Teachers have gone to Fiji and other
Pacific Islands, medical workers to Afghanistan, evangelists
and pastors to Britain.

* *Japan*. In the 1960s three young Japanese went to India
for theological study. Their purpose: to learn another
language and culture and prepare for overseas missionary
work. They went back to Japan, married three sisters and
scattered again to work in India and the Caribbean. Other
Japanese work today in Kenya, Indonesia, Nepal, Thailand,
Britain, and at least 20 other countries.

* *Korea*. A Korean girl works in London with Bengali
Muslims and Burmese Buddhists. A theological student is

now pastor to Korean businessmen in Bombay. A dentist has a clinic and plans for a dental college in Northern China. Koreans in the Middle East make an impression with their early morning prayer meetings.

* *Africans* cross national and cultural boundries within their continent. Kenyan students in India have a powerful witness. Nigerians and Ghanaians in Britain evangelize the local people. The East African Revival has ministered to people all round the world.

Robin Thomson, *World Christian*
(Lynx/St John's Extension Studies, 1992).

When we prioritize prayer we join with thousands of Christian men and women throughout history who have been used by God to accomplish great things in his name. There is no more important preparation for Christian service than having our character progressively made like Jesus through the ministry of prayer.

J. C. Ryle, a Bishop of Liverpool in the last century, summed it up like this: 'I have read the lives of many eminent Christians who have been on earth since the Bible days. Some of them, I see, were rich, and some were poor. Some were learned, some unlearned. Some have loved to use a liturgy, and some choose to use none. But

one thing, I see, they all had in common. They all
have been people of prayer.'

CHAPTER FIVE

READY TO GO?

KEY PASSAGES

Colossians 1:9–12, 28–29; 2:6–8

QUESTIONS FOR DISCUSSION

Re-read the section on 'maturing' (pp. 89–93) and the Scripture passages listed above.

1 Identify marks of maturity from these passages. How can you, as a group, specifically promote each other's growth in these areas?

2 Are there any areas in which you would particularly like to develop? (See leader's hint No. 1, p. 157, at the back of this book.)

3 What is the difference between being an 'older' Christian and being a 'more mature' Christian?

4 On page 89 we read 'Good relationship skills are very important in the task of mission.' Identify at least six such skills. In what ways can you develop in these skills?

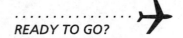

5 Is your group particularly strong or weak in any of these? Discuss your views about this together.

chapter six

A MISSION-MINDED CHURCH

··················

*'Foreign missions are not an extra; they are the
acid test of whether or not the church believes
the gospel.'*

Lesslie Newbiggin

··················

How can we get mission on to the agenda of the
local church? What should we do to give a
higher priority to the task of supporting mission
workers, being a mission-centred church and
producing interest in mission in our children and
young people?

BUDGET

Putting our money where our mouth is – that is
a good place to start. Many churches have taken
huge strides forward by making a significant
faith-decision about missionary giving. Some set

a 'goal per member'. That is, they pledge to give (say) £50 per member per year to mission, from the general fund (in other words, 100 members would generate £5,000 each year). Other churches decide to give a percentage of their annual income away. They may start by giving 10% and plan to increase this by a further 10% each year until, after five years, they are giving half of their income to 'outside causes'. Others go for more modest increases.

However it is done, it should be done! Only by giving decisively and generously can we avoid failing in our financial responsibilities in this area. 'In house' needs will always be present but we must resist using the mission budget to help balance the books. For many churches, publishing a minimum figure which they will give away is the only way to ensure that other claims don't eat into it each year. It's not unknown for a church treasurer to delay payment to a missionary society to the next financial year, or not to send it at all, when he's having trouble balancing the books! It is essential for local churches to move mission giving from the 'might pay' to the 'must pay' category!

This systematic and planned mission budgeting also helps avoid 'panic' or 'emotional' giving whenever a crisis occurs. Special collections and retiring offerings may have their place, but there are quickly diminishing returns if you do them too frequently. What's more, they tend to link mission support to a knee-jerk crisis mentality of giving. Mission should be supported because it is *right* to do all year round; not just because a big story hits our TV screens or a mission agency writes of a 'cash flow' crisis or a once-in-a-lifetime opportunity.

LEADERSHIP IN MISSION

Churches tend to reflect the priorities of their leaders. Whenever the minister is enthusiastic about mission, there is a good chance that the church will catch the vision. In an ideal situation, the leadership will be committed to seeing all of church life exposed to mission. This rescues mission from simply being the responsibility of yet another committee or pressure group in church life. It is, rather, the 'salt' of church life, flavouring everything, or, as a great Swiss theologian, Emil Brunner, put it, 'The church exists by mission, as fire exists by burning.'

Whether the minister of a church is positive about mission or not, the appointment of a mission co-ordinator or mission secretary can be very helpful. This individual should work under the authority of the church leadership, using every opportunity to stimulate interest in mission.

A mission co-ordinator in the church could be involved in:

* Running a monthly prayer meeting to pray for specific projects, organizations or countries. This prayer group could also be an action group, helping with other mission events.

* Write articles on mission for the church magazine. Review books about mission and ask the church bookstall to have a supply.

* Arrange an evening meal based around food from different countries. Pray for the countries. Have information sheets available on the tables. Play music from another culture. Have the waiters in national costumes. Write the menu in various languages. With some imagination, this can be a very enjoyable evening and can significantly affect mission prayer and interest.

* Put up a mission display board. Give information about a missionary or a country. List items for praise and needs for prayer. Lots of big pictures, a map, diagrams and bright colours are ideal. Keep it simple and uncluttered, with not too many words in small type. Change it every month if you can. Be as professional as possible.

* Inform house groups. Perhaps you could send material to house group leaders from time to time, giving prayer information. Try to let them know what happened as a result of their prayers!

* Ask the leaders for a specific prayer and information slot during occasional Sunday services. Be brief, specific and interesting – especially if you want to be allowed to do it again! Use the overhead projector or show a piece of clothing from the relevant country or bring a national flag. Encourage your leaders to include some aspect of mission whenever God's people get together.

* See if you can arrange a mission weekend. This could involve seminars on the Saturday, on mission-related topics. A guest speaker could be invited for the Sunday services. Decorate the church with a variety of national flags. Learn a song or hymn from another country. Have a number of displays featuring the work of various mission agencies.

* Consider twinning your church with another fellowship in a completely different part of the world. You could exchange news-letters, prayer topics, even pastors (temporarily!) to ensure greater understanding of the world church. You could send money or personnel to help support them in specific projects.

SUPPORTING MISSIONARIES

If someone has gone from your church family to do Christian service – whether at home or abroad – you will want to support them as well as possible. If no-one has gone from your church you could 'adopt' a mission worker serving in a part of the world you want to pray for. A mission agency could help provide you with someone to 'adopt'.

Either way, the mission worker you are linked with will want to know that he or she is supported in *prayer*. Not just promises of prayer, but the real thing! One of the saddest stories I have heard was about a missionary couple and their young child who felt called to a particularly difficult part of Africa. The whole church cove-nanted to pray for them – especially about the threat to their lives from disease and marauding gangs. After less than two years the little boy and his mother died of a virulent local fever and the husband too became infected. He was rushed back to his home country in a last ditch attempt to save his life. Discharged from hospital, for there was little the doctors could do, he arrived late for the church prayer meeting. Slipping in at the back, he sat unnoticed through the whole meeting. There were prayers for many aspects of church life, but not a mention of him or his situation, despite his letters urging prayer for his family in crisis. He slipped quietly out into the night, forgotten by everyone but God. He died within days, a broken, crushed man. A brother betrayed by unkept promises! This is a stark reminder to say what we mean, and mean what we say about praying for mission workers.

....

'Unprayed for I feel like a diver at the bottom of a river with no connecting airline to the surface, or like a fireman wielding an empty hose on a burning building. With prayer I feel like David facing Goliath.'

James Gilmour, missionary to Mongolia

....

And, of course, mission workers need to be supported *financially*. If there is a sending agency (such as a missionary society or evangelistic organization) some discussion will need to take place with them. What level of support is needed? How long is the appointment for? What happens if the money runs out? Whatever the precise details of the arrangements the local church will want to be as generous as possible.

Missionaries also need *contact* support. They could be sent tapes of the services, the church news-letter and perhaps a monthly precis of key developments in church life. Church members should be encouraged to write, fax or phone, as appropriate. From time to time a significant new Christian book could be posted to them or the latest tape of worship songs. Try to imagine what you would miss if you lived for long periods abroad! Would they appreciate a subscription to a sport or hobbies magazine? A newspaper? A supply of liquorice allsorts? Try especially to remember birthdays and anniversaries. Be creative and energetic in discovering and meeting these personal needs. A taken-for-granted item here, in the West, can make a huge difference to someone thousands of miles away from home!

The key to supporting workers in mission – in prayer, finance and contact – is consistency. Mission support is a marathon, not a sprint. 'Little and often' is a much better approach than overwhelming support for two months, followed by two years of virtual silence!

When they come home

* Welcome returning missionaries with enthusiasm. Make them feel appreciated and loved. Perhaps you should send a 'welcoming committee' to the airport. But give them space to get over jet-lag and re-acclimatize to life back home.

* Give them an early and significant opportunity to address the church with a word of greeting and news highlights. After a few weeks an opportunity can be arranged for a fuller report to be given, and time set aside to pray. Let them tell their story.

* Give thought to questions related to where they might live while on home assignment, and their need for a car – before they come home! Will they need extra money while they are home?

* Things have changed while they were away! The church might consider appointing a (discreet, gentle and thoughtful) 'minder' to provide appropriate phone numbers, directions to new facilities and an escort on shopping outings and so on.

* Be sensitive! Coming home can be a huge emotional adjustment. Meeting up with family they may not have seen for a couple of years; sad to be away from their colleagues on the mission field; overwhelmed by the affluence of the West compared with where they have been . . . These, and many other things, can be quite a shock to the system.

* What do they enjoy doing which it is hard to do abroad? Watch Manchester United? See a West End play? Visit a stately home? Perhaps the church could find out and provide the money and contacts to make it happen.

* Why not suggest (and pay for!) a complete medical examination for the missionary family? A visit to the dentist? An optician's appointment? Health-care overseas may not always be good, and you do want to send your Christian workers back in the best possible shape!

* Representatives of the leadership should meet with returning workers to discuss support, links with their sending agency and to give both sides time to reflect on how to strengthen missionary–church links. There may be unrealized expectations and frustrations on either/both sides of this discussion. Honesty, love and sensitivity will be needed!

* Try to treat them 'normally'. Make sure they are included in routine church life; not as special guests, just as part of the family. Don't give them a special welcome at every meeting or fuss over them in an unnaturally gushing way. This can appear to be condescending or patronizing – 'our sweet little missionary family'!

* Give them the opportunity to attend refresher courses, and to engage in extra study to prepare them for their next term of service.

* Send them back with prayer, perhaps in a special service of re-commissioning. Give a small gift to each member of the family, to take as a reminder of the love and prayers of the people back home. Arrange for them to be taken to the airport.

A MISSION–CHURCH: TODAY AND TOMORROW

It is vital to infect future generations with the mission-enthusiasm bug! Our children's programme and activities should reflect a passion for world mission. Returning Christian workers should not be viewed as the exclusive property of the 'adult church'. Simple concepts illustrated with striking visual aids can draw even very young children into the world of mission. Perhaps a serving missionary could write a 'child-friendly' news-letter, or the grown-ups' version could be adapted by a children's worker. Curriculum materials should include illustrations from other cultures. Some mission agencies produce magazines for children and these can be circulated and could form part of a lesson in Junior Church, Sunday School, or Christian Education.

Many churches have the world on their own doorsteps! What about a joint session with the children from the Chinese Church down the road? Or a visit from a West Indian children's choir? Experiences like these broaden our children's understanding of culture and Christian faith. There is an important challenge here for the children's workers and helpers in our churches. We must take great care not to pass on to our children our own prejudices or misconceptions about people of other races and nationalities. Views which imply a cultural superiority, or subtle racism, are not unknown in our churches!

Where we have Christian parents, this is obviously the best place to foster world-mission awareness – in the home. We can make a point of entertaining Christian workers for Sunday lunch, whenever the opportunity arises. We can support in an active way all the mission emphases to which the church is trying to expose our children. If you get hold of a copy of *You Can Change the World* (OM Publishing, 1993) you will be able to talk and pray with your children about dozens of different nations of the world. Children tend to pick up our values and priorities through the routine atmosphere of life in the home. What we give time to, spend money on and talk about, all send signals which shape young lives.

Once they get to the pocket-money stage, it can be useful to encourage them to give a proportion to the church, and another sum specifically for world mission. A map of the world in the hallway or a globe on top of the piano can be a useful visual reminder of life beyond the home country. Write a family letter to a mission worker, with each family member contributing. The youngest child could draw a picture or at least make a mark on the paper – a missionary family would relate to this correspondence with enthusiasm!

The role of the church is to encourage parents to take their world-mission responsibilities to their children seriously. We may even be able to arrange a 'missionary experience' at the church (such as displays, mission literature, food-tasting, a makeshift 'slum', border controls, games) which adults and children can tour together. In the long-term, we pray that these children will grow up with a world-mission focus firmly established as part of their Christian experience; ready, in turn, to pass on this commitment to mission to their own children.

Churches which do the kinds of things this chapter has described can make a significant contribution to global mission. Churches like this also tend to be making a significant impact locally. My observation over the years has been that when local congregations are absorbed with 'external' needs, 'internal' issues (such as worship and unity) are not major sources of contention. When a church is 'internally' focused, mission is neglected and 'internal' tensions absorb ever-increasing amounts of time and energy! Let's get our churches focused upwards to God and outwards to the world.

A MISSION-MINDED CHURCH

KEY PASSAGES

Philippians 1:3–5; 4:14–19

QUESTIONS FOR DISCUSSION

1 Which of the ideas presented in this chapter do you think it would be good for you/your family/your church to adopt? How can you make progress in this?

2 Re-read the section on 'supporting missionaries' (pp. 111–116). How could your group be directly involved in this?

3 Imagine a missionary from your church has just returned from ten years in Nepal. What cultural changes will they encounter? How can you make their re-entry go more smoothly (pp. 114–116)?

4 The Philippian church stood out to Paul as giving good support. How do you think their support affected Paul? What did they lose or gain by supporting him in the way they did?

5 To what extent is your church 'internally focused' or 'externally focused' (p. 119)? What can you/your group do to be more externally focused?

HEROES FOR A
WORLD IN NEED

This is a very needy world. We only need to watch the television news or listen to the reports on the car radio on the way to work. Our eyes and ears are exposed daily to a diet of death, disease, war and famine. Greed on a global scale, searing anger and hatred between individuals and nations – an almost constant shroud of sadness seems to cover our broken world. Of course, there is also evidence of hope in the most unlikely places. Costly acts of kindness, self-sacrificing compassion and deep expressions of love – all these things exist in far greater quantity than ever gets a mention on the national news! Some hungry people are fed, some homeless people are housed and some defenceless people are protected. Christians are actively involved, with others, in these vital activities.

And the gospel is making inroads into our world. About 40 million people become Christians each year and some 50,000 churches are planted. In parts of Africa the church is growing faster than the population. South Korea is on course for half its population to be Christians! On every continent (with the exception of Europe!) the church of Jesus seems to be growing. This information should encourage us, but not cause us to be complacent. These signs of hope should not obscure the size of the task which remains to be done.

___

Where are the lost?

* Most of those who have not heard the gospel are in the 10/40 window. This is an area from 10 degrees north latitude to 40 degrees north latitude, and covers much of northern Africa, the Arab world, India, China and Indonesia.

* This area has over 4 billion people which includes 1 billion Muslims, 1 billion Hindus and 237 million Buddhists.

* 8 out of 10 of the world's poor live here.

* 50 of the least evangelized cities (1 million people plus) are in the window.

* It attracts only 20% of missionary resources.

Dave Roberts, *Mission Possible* (Evangelical Missionary Alliance/Alpha Magazine, 1994).

___

Around 40% of the population of planet earth (approximately two billion people) have still to hear the gospel in a way they can understand. Islam may be spreading at an even more rapid rate than Christianity; and Hinduism at an equal rate with the Christian faith.

Secularization continues to engulf the affluent West with a consequent abandonment of traditional forms of Christianity. New-Age teaching abounds and the cults continue to flourish. 90% of preachers are working with the 10% of the world's population who speak English. Only 0.6% of full-time missionaries are working among people-groups where the good news is completely unknown. There are still over 3,000 languages with no access to any part of the Bible and a quarter of all people-groups don't have a meaningful church to be part of. Giving to missionary agencies is rising more slowly than inflation, and I wouldn't be at all surprised if more Christians buy National Lottery tickets than give to the mission task abroad!

There is still a great deal to be done. Population growth alone gives us a huge task, well into the next century. And much of this growth will be in China and India, where the gospel has not found it easy to make progress. Perhaps the task we face is not greater than in the past, but mission workers today face different problems. Transport and communication, two of the

greatest practical problems facing past generations of missionaries, are much easier today;
almost everywhere physical danger, health risks
and poor living conditions may all have been
more of a problem than they are today. Separation from family and friends was for longer
periods, sometimes indefinitely! Amy Carmichael was in India for fifty-three years without
a break! William Carey *never* came home on
furlough. Missionary news could take six months
or longer to get back to Britain. And don't
forget, the concept of short-term missionary
service is a very recent one. It only became
possible with the arrival of relatively cheap
passenger air travel.

Mission in the '90s

Mission in the '90s is a million miles removed from images of
pith helmets and mission compounds. What has changed?

National leadership
Mission groups seek to work themselves out of a job by
relinquishing power as soon as possible to local leadership.
This creates faster church growth, causes less communication
problems and negates the possibility of any unhealthy
cultural imperialism.

Targeting people-groups
There may be 251 nations in the world but there are at least 12,000 people-groups with their own distinctive culture, customs and language forms. 5,000 of the least reached groups are in the 10/40 window (see p. 124). Pioneer cross-cultural missionaries are still needed to help these groups. These pioneers will be needed for several decades as they seek to support new local leadership with Bible and mission training.

Wholistic mission
While some mission groups emphasize church planting, others also emphasize that the kingdom of God means justice for the oppressed and food for the hungry. Many believe that there is not an either/or tension and we need to both plant churches and promote justice.

The multi-cultural church
The meteoric rise of vibrant Christianity in Latin America, Korea and various other communities worldwide means that western Christians no longer dominate the worldwide Christian community.

Non-white believers are now in the worldwide majority. It's estimated that the 35,000 non-western missionaries of the late '80s will have multiplied to a 160,000 majority group in world mission by the year 2000.

Church to church
To help western Christians retain a passion for mission, creative strategies of involvement are being pursued.

Church twinning is bringing together churches like the Christian Fellowship Church in Belfast and the Tabernacle Church in Madrid. Some churches, if they're ready for the long haul, are getting involved in pioneer people-group evangelism. Often they are working closely with a mission agency to help research mission opportunities during holidays, student visits and business trips to the relevant area. When a church has been established they 'twin' with the church and help support them in practical and spiritual ways.

With a broad cross-section of the congregation involved in what is essentially a long-distance church plant taking place, the needs of mission, and its impact, become very tangible to the home church.

World mission is alive and well. There's a commitment to cultural sensitivity and a desire to stay only as long as a missionary is needed. There's a passion for the lost and a passion for justice. There are ample opportunities for local Christians to think globally.

Source: Dave Roberts, *Mission Possible* (Evangelical Missionary Alliance/Alpha Magazine, 1994).

Despite all this, women and men did risk everything in response to the call of God to share the good news – heroes of the faith. Their lives, warts and all, have a good deal to teach us today.

HEROES WHO NEVER GAVE UP

....

'I know exactly what you are going through because I am going through the same thing . . . It seems as though everything I do is wrong and only my faith in a living God keeps me going, because I get one bang after another.'

Gladys Aylward

....

To read some biographies of missionaries you would think they arrived on foreign soil, led thousands to Christ, planted dozens of churches and died famous and appreciated! In reality, most godly missionaries are characterized by faithfulness and dogged stickability; people who would never give up until God called them elsewhere or until they died.

William Carey endured incredible hardship in India. Peter, his five-year-old son, died. Dorothy, his wife, went mad and died. He re-married and his second wife died. His books were destroyed in a fire, including a translation of the Bible which he had to begin again.

C. T. Studd went as a missionary to China in 1885. After nine years, ill-health forced him to return home. In 1900 he went to India, until sickness again saw him back in Britain. In 1910 (contrary to medical advice) he went to Africa, where he worked until he died in 1931.

Amy Carmichael suffered a dislocated ankle, broken leg and twisted spine. So bad were these injuries that between 1931 (when the accident occurred) and 1939 she only had eight nights of sleep without the help of medication for the pain. And all the while she was running her children's home in India, suffering intermittent bouts of fever and neuralgia!

John Ryle, in his later ministry a very influential Bishop of Liverpool, had to persist through many early trials. He spent his first years of ministry burdened with a huge family debt. His ministry was overshadowed by a wealthy aggressive layman who wished to run the church, causing John much heartache. During this same ministry he buried his first wife in 1847 and his second wife in 1860. Personal bereavement and professional hardship ran side by side.

More recently, Jackie Pullinger persevered for many years working with the hungry and the drug addicts of Hong Kong. The need was desperate and there was so little that she felt she could do. Now there are teams reaching where she could not go.

As I write, 'jungle missionaries' work in the Peruvian Amazon, staying one step ahead of terrorists, drug traffickers, and oil men, who are devastating jungle society and threatening its survival. Native missionaries like Roger and

Rebeca Márquez are involved in jungle mission, motivating local tribal village churches in outreach. Native evangelists have preached the gospel in every one of the villages of the Shipibo tribe. Both Roger and Rebecca received a missionary calling to the Peruvian Amazon. The difficulties are great and the costs high – one native evangelist died from a poisonous snake bite while going to preach at an unreached village.

For all these people, faith and Christian ministry did not come easily. They proved the truth that 'successful people are unsuccessful people who didn't give up'. The mission task still needs people who will not give up!

. . . .

President Roosevelt said: 'Since becoming President, I have come to know that the finest of Americans we have abroad today are the missionaries of the Cross. I am humiliated that I am not finding out until this late day the worth of foreign missions and the nobility of the missionaries. Their testimony in China, for instance, during the war there, is beyond praise. Their courage is thrilling and their fortitude heroic.'

. . . .

HEROES IN THE RIGHT PLACE – EVENTUALLY

We often imagine that guidance comes easily to Christian workers. Don't they all have a hotline to heaven telling them where to work, when, and how to get there? Actually they are often as confused as we are! David Livingstone first thought God was calling him to China – and then went to Africa. William Carey felt he should serve God in Tahiti – and ended up in India. And as for Thomas Barnado – he felt sure that God wanted him in China. He had come from Dublin to London to train as a missionary doctor. While in preparation to go he started a meeting for 'street-children' in the East End of London. After one of these meetings one of the poorest of the boys simply would not go home. Jim Jarvis told Barnado that he had no home to go to! Barnado could hardly believe it. Soon after this he met Lord Shaftsbury at a dinner party and told him about the homelessness and poverty in the East End. Anthony Shaftsbury did not believe him until he was taken by Barnado himself to a warehouse in Whitechapel. Here he encountered seventy-three boys living rough! 'Are you sure that it is to China God is sending you?' Something 'clicked' inside Thomas Barnado and he devoted his life to the needy in London instead of China. This happened in 1866.

In the thirty-nine years to his death his organization admitted 59,384 children to his homes and helped a quarter of a million others!

China's loss was London's gain. Thank God that mission work is not closed to those who struggle with guidance, perhaps even getting it wrong at first.

UNLIKELY HEROES

Another myth about missionary 'greats' is that somehow they had special advantages we lack – wasn't Barnado from a wealthy, well-connected family? Wasn't John Wesley a graduate of Oxford University? Didn't C. T. Studd have the privilege of attending Eton and then Cambridge University? Yes, all this is true, but not necessarily typical! William Carey was a shoemaker with almost no formal education – what he learnt he taught himself. Robert Moffat was an apprentice gardener who struggled to get himself accepted by a missionary society. He went on to have a huge impact in Africa, and was the inspiration which drew David Livingstone to that country! Mary Slessor had a very difficult home life; they were extremely poor and her father was an alcoholic. She had very little education yet God used her to have a profound impact in Nigeria – far greater than anyone could ever imagine or have thought possible, given her background. Her influence continues there to this day.

And what about Gladys Aylward? She had a significant impact in China; sharing the gospel, caring for the needy and looking after refugees. On one incredible occasion she took over one hundred children on a 200-mile journey over mountainous terrain to avoid capture by an invading army. And all this from a woman who was consistently bottom of her class at school, could find employment only as a maid in a wealthy household and was turned down by the missionary society she applied to, because they did not believe she would ever be able to learn Chinese!

The history of mission is a colourful history of 'unlikely heroes' – characterized by obedience rather than ability. Time after time God confirms his Word; 'Think of what you were when you were called. Not many of you were wise by human standards; not many were influential; not many were of noble birth. But God chose the foolish things of the world to shame the wise; God chose the weak things of the world to shame the strong' (1 Corinthians 1:26–27).

What makes a hero?

The model of a hero for a Christian is the hero of heroes, Jesus, who, though he was God, voluntarily stripped himself of power, success and influence, steadfastly setting his face towards his sacrificial death in Jerusalem. He became a humble carpenter-builder, whose disciples were made up of fishermen and social outcasts.

The Bible is a gallery of unlikely heroes; men and women with obvious faults and feet of clay, who nevertheless had the courage to endure in faith. They had the character to overcome, sometimes intermittently, the limitations of their backgrounds, to renounce the ways of the powerful in favour of faith in God's plans, however foolish these plans seemed to the powerful (see Hebrews 11).

A contemporary writer who has effectively portrayed heroes with biblical qualities of humility, perseverance and character is J. R. R. Tolkien, most well known for his *The Lord of the Rings*. His heroes include humble hobbits, half the height of mankind, and a king with healing hands who disguises himself for very many years as a wandering ranger. These heroes are guided by an unseen providence and their renunciation of power, and sacrifice, outwits the dark power who holds the world in his sway.

UNSUNG HEROES

And the history of mission is not primarily a story of 'famous' people. Thousands of unknown women and men have laid down their lives in God's service. In fact, when God records the story of the world church, names you have never heard of will be given high profile and some 'famous' Christians may hardly get a mention! For example, you have probably never heard of Edward Kimball, yet he set in process a remarkable chain of events because of his faithful 'missionary' service.

Edward Kimball sold shoes for a living. He also happened to be Dwight Moody's Sunday School teacher. One day in April 1858 he challenged Moody to give his life to Christ. Moody, who was working in his uncle's shoe shop, gave his life to God in the basement storeroom. He grew up to give the same challenge to hundreds of thousands of others – on both sides of the Atlantic. While preaching in England in 1879 he awakened the evangelistic passion of a pastor of a small church – his name was F. B. Meyer. Meyer came to America and saw a young student, Wilbur Chapman, won to the Lord. Chapman went to work for the Y.M.C.A. and asked Billy Sunday to help with the evangelism. Having cut his teeth evangelistically at the Y.M.C.A. Sunday went to hold an evangelistic campaign in

Charlotte, North Carolina. It went so well, a follow-up mission was arranged, with Mordecai Hamm as the evangelist. It was during this mission that a sixteen-year-old boy made a public decision to follow Jesus. His name? Billy Graham!

Billy Graham has preached the good news to more people than anyone else in all of history. Edward Kimball could not have known how incredibly strategic his conversation with Moody would turn out to be. It could be argued that all those converted under Billy Graham's ministry owe a debt to Edward Kimball. Any one of us could be used to start a chain of events similar to this!

. . . .

'The evangelistic harvest is always urgent. The destiny of men and of nations is always being decided. Every generation is strategic. We are not responsible for the past generation, and we cannot bear the full responsibility for the next one; but we do have our generation. God will hold us responsible as to how well we fulfil our responsibilities to this age and take advantage of our opportunities.'

Billy Graham

. . . .

John Staupitz and John Egglen are completely unknown to the vast majority of Christians – yet they were the ones who were instrumental in leading Martin Luther and Charles Spurgeon, respectively, to Christian faith. Unknown? Yes, but absolutely vital in the unfolding purposes of God. Unsung heroes? Yes, by everyone except God!

George Verwer traces his conversion to the persistent prayers of an elderly woman for his high school. He went on to inspire tens of thousands of young people of all abilities to short-term and long-term mission through Operation Mobilization.

And, of course, there are thousands of others who have responded to God's call. These missionaries will never make it into the history books. You would be thrilled to know about Edwin who was called by God at thirty-nine years of age to Columbia. A farmer, knowing only two words of Spanish, he sold his farm, and went for twenty years before a brief visit home. He has made a tremendous contribution for God – and still works there in Columbia today. Or Dave who works in social work in the UK; or Valerie, a doctor, or Roger, an assembly-line worker, or Jane, a housewife, or – the list goes on and on. These people all have a passion for mission, and I'm sure have a place in God's book of 'missionary greats'. Why not join them and become one of God's twenty-first century heroes, your life marked, like theirs, with the struggles and joys of being a servant and mission agent for God?

CHAPTER SEVEN

HEROES FOR A WORLD IN NEED

KEY PASSAGES

1 Corinthians 1:26–27; Hebrews 12:1–4

QUESTIONS FOR DISCUSSION

1 What impressed itself on you as you read of the 'heroes' mentioned in this chapter?

2 To what extent are these heroes ordinary, to what extent extraordinary?

3 What things do they have in common?

4 How can you develop individually and as a group in these areas?

5 Re-read the story of Edward Kimball (p. 136). Do you think you could be an Edward Kimball? What can you do/pray, or ask others to do/pray, to help you be used by God in a similar way?

6 In the light of Billy Graham's comment
(p. 137) discuss together what is involved in
fulfilling your (individual and joint)
responsibilities to this generation.

AFTERWORD

So, despite my warning, you read the book! That was a big mistake, but all is not lost. I suppose you now believe that mission is very important indeed and that you must play your part in bringing the gospel to the world.

Well, that's fine, but let me give you a word of advice. This is far too important a subject to be rushed into without thinking. Why not put the book away for a few months, and then see how you feel about things? There really isn't any hurry. Your tiny contribution is hardly going to change the world, so no-one will worry if you delay making your contribution to world mission. You must think of your career, your financial security and your future plans – wouldn't it be better to get all these things sorted out before turning your attention to the ideas in this book?

And remember your image! No-one likes a fanatic. Over-keenness can be dangerous. Let's leave this passionate enthusiasm stuff for the sports arena or political rally. We don't want to put people off by our outspoken commitment to global evangelism – they might think we wanted to be as good as those early Christians the New Testament describes. Hell forbid!

So, just relax and let the fuss die down. Your future is guaranteed; don't worry about the others. I'll take care of them for you. There is no need for you to bother – I will!

Lucy Fer

Lucy Fer

RESOURCES

CONTENTS

1. KEY BOOKS ON MISSION

Betty Barnett, *Friend Raising: Building a missionary support team that lasts* (YWAM, 1991).

Anne Cooper (ed.), *Ishmael My Brother: A Christian Introduction to Islam* (Monarch Publications, 1993).

Wesley Duewel, *Touch the World Through Prayer* (Zondervan, 1986).

Michael Griffiths, *Tinker, Tailor, Missionary?: Options in a Changing World* (IVP/OM, 1992).

Patrick Johnstone, *Operation World* (OM Publishing, 1993).

Ted Lankester, *Good Health, Good Travel* (Hodder & Stoughton, 1995).

Philip Mohabir, *Worlds Within Reach* (Hodder & Stoughton, 1992).

Glenn Myers, *The World Christian Starter Kit*, (WEC/OM, 1993).

Ross Paterson, *Explaining Mission* (Sovereign World, 1993).

John Piper, *Let the Nations be Glad* (IVP, 1994).

Neal Pirolo, *Serving as Senders* (Emmaus Road International, 1991).

Don Richardson, *Eternity in Their Hearts* (Regal Books, 1981).

Robin Thomson, *World Christian* (Lynx/St John's Extension Studies, 1992).

Chris Wright, *What's So Unique About Jesus?* (ANCC/Monarch Publications, 1990).

For Children:
Jill Johnstone, *You Can Change the World* (OM Publishing, 1993).
You Can Change the World Activity Pack (OM Publishing, 1993).

2. MISSION BIOGRAPHIES

Dick Anderson, *We felt like grasshoppers* (Crossway, 1994).
Eileen Crossman, *Mountain Rain* (OMF, 1988).
Elisabeth Elliot, *A Chance to Die: The life of Amy Carmichael* (OM, 1994).
——, *Shadow of the Almighty* (OM, 1988)
——, *Through gates of splendour* (OM, 1988).
Timothy George, *Faithful Witness: life and mission of William Carey* (IVP, 1992).
Isobel Kuhn, *Green leaf in drought* (OMF, 1986).
——, *Nests above the abyss* (OMF, 1988).
——, *Stones of fire* (OMF, 1989).
Sally Magnusson, *The Flying Scotsman: Biography of Eric Liddell* (Quartet Books, 1981).
Steven Masood, *Into the light* (OM, 1992).
Malcolm Muggeridge, *Something beautiful for God* (Fount, 1972).
John Pollock, *The Cambridge Seven* (IVP, 1995).
Jackie Pullinger, *Chasing the dragon* (Hodder & Stoughton, 1980).

——, *Crack in the wall* (Hodder & Stoughton, 1989).

Helen Roseveare, *Give me this mountain* (IVP, 1994).

——, *He gave us a valley* (IVP, 1994).

Stuart Sendall-King, *Hope has wings: The Mission Aviation Fellowship story* (Marshall Pickering, 1993).

Mrs Howard Taylor, *Biography of James Hudson Taylor* (Hodder & Stoughton, 1973).

——, *Pastor Hsi* (OMF, 1989).

Phyllis Thompson, *Sadhu Sundar Singh* (OM, 1992).

John Waters, *David Livingstone: Trail Blazer* (IVP, 1996).

3. AUDIO VISUALS

World Outreach Resource Material Catalogue (WORM) (Evangelical Missionary Alliance, 1993).

Producers of videos and audio material, listed in WORM, include the following:

Interserve, 325 Kennington Road, London, SE11 4QH, UK.

Society for International Ministries (SIM), Joint Mission Centre, Ullswater Crescent, Croydon, CR5 2HR, UK.

UFM Worldwide, 47a Fleet Street, Swindon, Wiltshire, SN1 1RE, UK.

Tear Fund, 100 Church Road, Teddington, Middlesex, TW11 8QE, UK.

WEC International, Bulstrode, Oxford Road, Gerrards Cross, Buckinghamshire, SL9 8SZ, UK.

Wycliffe Bible Translators, Horsleys Green, High Wycombe, Buckinghamshire, HP14 3XL, UK.

4. PRAYER RESOURCES

World Prayer News (published by EMA).
Operation World Prayer Cards (available from all good Christian bookshops).
Fellowship of Faith for the Muslims, PO Box 1307, Worthing, West Sussex, BN14 8JS.

5. KEY RESOURCE GROUPS IN THE UK

Evangelical Missionary Alliance, Whitefield House, 186 Kennington Park Road, London SE11 4BT. Tel. 0171 207 2156.
(For general enquiries related to who works where and how to link up with mission agencies.)

Christian Service Centre, Holloway Street West, Lower Gornal, Dudley, West Midlands, DY3 2DZ. Tel: 01902 882836.
(For details about job opportunities both long term and short term. They publish 'Jobs Abroad' and 'Short Term Service Directory'.)

Interhealth, Partnership House, 157 Waterloo Road, London SE1 8UU. Tel: 0171 902 9000.

Evangelical Alliance World Mission Secretary, Whitefield House, 186 Kennington Park Road, London SE11 4BT. Tel: 0171 207 2100.

6. RESOURCE GROUPS IN OTHER COUNTRIES

Missions Interlink, PO Box 581, New Farm, Queensland, Australia 4005.

Mission Internet, PO Box 27–548, Mt. Roskill, Auckland, New Zealand.

Centre for Mission Direction, PO Box 31146, 70 Norton's Road, Christchurch, New Zealand.

EZA, Eendrachstraat 29a, 3784 KA Terschuur, Netherlands.

Association of Evangelicals of Africa, PO Box 49332, Nairobi, Kenya.

European Evangelical Alliance, Postfach 23, 1037 Vienna, Austria.

India Missions Association, 48 First Main Road, East Shenoynagar, Madras -600 030, India.

AEM, Hindenburgstr 36, 70825 Korntal-Munch-ingen, Germany.

Comibam International, Apdo. Postal 27-1, CP 1907, Guatemala, C. America.

Singapore Centre for Evangelism & Missions, 116 Lavendar Street, #04-07 Pek Chuan Building, Singapore 1233.

7. TRAINING

Association of Bible College Principals, c/o Moor-lands College, Sopley, Christchurch, Dorset, BH23 7AT.

Perspectives Courses, Contact person: Rev. Richard Tiplady, 12 Priory Drive, Hull, N. Hum-berside, HU5 5UA.

Culture to Culture Courses, St John's Extension Studies, Chilwell Lane, Bramcote, Nottingham, NG9 3DS.

World Mission and the Local Church; Neighbours Pack, Evangelical Alliance, Whitefield House, 186 Kennington Park Road, London SE11 4BT.

8. SAMPLE APPLICATION FORM

Long-term Christian Service

Application form
Name
Address
Date of birth
Marital status
Do you possess a full driving license?
Educational background and academic qualifications.
List your previous employers and work experience.
How did you become a Christian?
Which church do you attend?
Are your church leaders supportive of your application?
Describe the precise way by which you were called to full-time Christian work.
Why do you want to serve with this particular organization?
What Christian work or ministry are you involved in already in your local church?

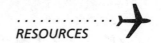
What Christian books have you read in the last year?
Which do you find most helpful?
Do you speak a foreign language?
What contacts have you had in other countries?
Do you have a current passport?
What hobbies or recreational activities are you involved in?
Can you provide three references in support of your application?

In addition to this, there will undoubtedly be questions about your emotional and psychological stability. You will be asked to provide a number of passport size photographs and probably be required to sign a Statement of Faith. There may also be an opportunity to write at greater length on a number of foundational biblical topics.

---

9. GROUP LEADER'S HINTS

Chapter 1: Becoming a world Christian

1 If your group is geographically based, set the group the task of finding out as much as they can about the locality. Use a future meeting to collate the information and use it as a basis for prayer and action. You can do the same for any part of the world.

2 Use the ideas on page 18 to compose a group letter to a missionary known to the group. Circulate paper and pens and give members of the group time to make their contributions. You might do the same with a cassette or even a video and send it to them.

Chapter 2: The ultimate authority

1 Open up the discussion first by allowing several people to contribute their answers before homing in on any particular point. Record the answers on a (flipchart) sheet of paper, then choose from these answers to focus and develop the issues.

2 Always try to ask 'open' questions (ones which allow more than one answer). Then let more than one answer be given.

Chapter 3: What is a missionary?

1 Encourage members of your group to tell their stories. Get the group to draw out the principles of telling, demonstrating and encountering from these stories. Aim to show how involvement in these actions is within reach of everyone in the group.

2 Keep the discussion moving around the group by asking different group members to build on the ideas shared by others. This also keeps group members listening to each other.

Chapter 4: Who will go?

1 Begin your discussion by dividing the group into threes and ask them to draw up a list of basic qualifications for missionary service. Have the groups feedback onto a 'master list'. Put a 'C' beside those relating to the quality of the person's character. Compare your list to Hudson Taylor's on page 75.

2 It may be that someone in your group will sense God nudging them to go. If so, pause and have the group pray with them about this. You might want to have a time of quiet in which people reflect on their own willingness to go.

3 New or quiet members of the group can be encouraged to participate by reading out the key passages for the group. If they are new to the Bible, point out the passage before the discussion starts.

Chapter 5: Ready to go?

1 Have different group members offer their area, then explore as a group what to do to help them develop. Don't forget to share yourself – you are part of the group.

2 Try to pursue people's answers by giving specific feedback or asking a follow-up question. For example, if 'listening to people' is mentioned as a skill, ask something like: 'How do I know if you are listening to me?'

3 Always receive people's contributions positively, even if you disagree with them. A simple 'good' or 'thank you for that' doesn't cost much, but goes a long way to encourage more contributions.

Chapter 6: A mission-minded church

1 To prevent this session from becoming over critical, concentrate on those issues within the sphere of influence of your group. Have a suggestions sheet which you can pass on to your church leaders.

2 Try having a brainstorming session to generate ideas for creative contact support of a missionary known to your group (pp. 113–114).

In a brainstorming session all contributions are accepted and recorded (no matter how off-beat or unworkable). No judgments are made or discussion had. The purpose is to get the group's creative juices flowing.

Chapter 7: Heroes for a world in need

1 Spend some time considering those unbelievers known to you and your group. Use the account of Edward Kimball to stimulate imaginative prayer for the influence of group members on the world through their relationships with these unbelievers.

2 Try to vary the style and interaction in group times. Have some time in pairs or threes as well as time all together.

The hints and study questions in this book were prepared by Phil Cuthbert.

Explaining Your Faith
(without losing your friends)
ALISTER McGRATH

You want to tell your non-Christian friends how exciting and relevant Christianity is. But what do you say?

Christian faith looks very different from the outside looking in! How can you explain it so that it makes sense to your friends?

Alister McGrath's book provides a straightforward, readable and intelligible account of what Christians believe – and why they believe it. He takes key topics that often come up in discussions, and shows how to explain them clearly.

160 pages   *Pocketbook*

Inter-Varsity Press